GREEN LIVING
BY DESIGN

GREEN LIVING BY DESIGN

The Practical Guide for Eco-Friendly Remodeling and Decorating

BY JEAN NAYAR

POINTCLICK**HOME**

PHOTO CREDITS

American Standard: 85; Avonite: 112 (top left); Lincoln Barbour: 56 (bottom left), 83, 90, 94, 96, 109; Bark House: 51 (top right); Benjamin Moore: 107 (right); Biokleen: 146 (right); Bulthaup: 115 (top right); CaesarStone: 113 (bottom right); Caperton: 133 (bottom left); Caroma: 85 (top right); Cisco Brothers: 137 (middle left); C.R. Laine: 137 (middle right); Grey Crawford: 71; Sarah Dorio: 35; Casey Dunn: 10, 60–61, 142–143; The Container Store: 149 (bottom right); Eagle Roofing Products: 69; EcoSmart Fire: 73 (bottom left); Ecosourceline: 36 (bottom left); EcoTimber: 119 (bottom); J. Savage Gibson: 2; Tria Giovan: 6; David Groul: 45, 53, 76; John Gruen: 141 (all); Ken Gutmaker: 93, 122, 147; Anastasia Harrison: page 18, 46, 73 (top right), 119 (top), 155, 157; Habitat for Humanity: 148; Hickory Chair Company: 132 (top, bottom), 133 (right); Erik Johnson: 92; Rob Kern: 13 (top right), 16–17, 56 (top right), 75, 99, 104, 118 (top right), 144; Hulya Kolabas: 107; Lee Industries: 134, 137 (top right); Chris Little: 11 (right), 102–103, 111, 114 (bottom), 127, 130, 138; David Duncan Livingston: 91; Maison Belle: 146 (left); Steven Mays: 8–9, 12 (left), 30, 38–39, 41, 84, 89, 95, 101, 106, 113 (top right), 114 (top), 140; Moen: 85 (bottom right); Keith Scott Morton: 28–29, 79, 105, 129, 131, 136 (left), 150; NatureMill: 153 (bottom); Emily Minton Redfield: 115; Bruce Nelson: 33 (top right); Michael Partenio: 124–125; Marisa Pellegrini: 78, 117, 135, 149 (top right); Eric Piasecki: 116; Plyboo: 115 (top left); Pure Furniture: 128, 136 (right); Mariko Reed: 24, 32, 36 (top left), 57, 71, 72, 80, 85 (left middle), 118 (bottom left); Jay Rosenblatt: 11(left), 20, 22–23, 27, 37, 44, 49, 50, 51 (top left), 58, 63, 87, 97, 112, 149 (top left), 151, 156; Rowe Furniture: 137 (top left and bottom center); Smith & Hawken: 153 (top); Jamie Solomon: 34, 66, 68, 110, 121, 126; Susan Sully: 13 (bottom right), 139; John Swain: 82; Terracycle: 33 (bottom left); The Old Wood Co.: 133 (top left); Paul Warchol: 12 (left), 31, 51 (bottom right), 54, 64, 70, 107 (left).

First published in 2009 in the United States of America by Filipacchi Publishing
1633 Broadway
New York, NY 10019

PointClickHome.com is a registered trademark of Hachette Filipacchi Media U.S., Inc.

Design: Patricia Fabricant
Editing: Lauren Kuczala
Production: Ed Barredo

ISBN 13: 978-1-933231-53-2

Library of Congress Control Number: 2008937592

Printed in China on recycled paper.

CONTENTS

FOREWORD

In 1983, my family and I built a vacation home in the Pocono Mountains with material salvaged from a building my father demolished in Philadelphia. Massive wood beams, reclaimed framing lumber, steel, even nails were reused and reconfigured to make what I think of as our first "sustainable" building, though we didn't think of it as such at the time.

This was an important lesson to learn as a first-year architecture student. The essence of living and building "green," for us, has always been about living and building thoughtfully, creatively, efficiently and sensibly. We have never considered "green" living as an alternative lifestyle or our buildings as novelty products. We think of them as commonplace and common sense. Considering the impact of global warming on our planet, the fluctuation in non renewable fuel costs, the impact of the wars fought to protect those non renewable resources and national security threats as a result of such wars, one begins to wonder if we have forgotten the meaning of common sense. The question is not *What is the cost of "living green"?*, but rather *What is the cost of living otherwise?*

My brothers, a lifelong friend and I run a small and energetic development, design and construction company in Philadelphia and have, since 1997, worked and lived by the fundamental precept that "green" design is first and most importantl "great" design, and that great design does not have to cost more than poor design. Poor design is simply design that doesn't respond appropriately to one's environment—we think of it as "ir-responsible." On the other hand, "response-ability" in design might simply involve orienting a building respectfully and effectively on its site, or thoughtfully bringing natural light and ventilation into a room, or putting a garden on one's roof (we call it a "groof") to reduce heating/cooling loads and storm-water runoff and double the outdoor garden space of the site. It could also mean planting low-maintenance, drought-tolerant and native plants around your home, or heating a floor surface (and therefore your body) rather than a volume of space (and therefore your head). It could be as simple as using paints and sealants that don't contain harmful chemicals or working with materials and people that are local, or it could involve long-term approaches, such as collecting rainwater and reusing it to irrigate your lawn, or generating heat and power from the sun for free rather than paying for it from a coal burning utility company. These all seem like intelligent, rational, cost-effective and "natural" ways of being, thinking and designing, don't they?

For architects, these kinds of ideas are woven into the fabric of what we do on a daily basis. But for the rest of the world, sorting through the ever-evolving ways in which one chooses to live a greener life can be challenging at best. So a clearly organized, informed book such as *Green Living by Design* helps us bridge the gaps in the ways we communicate, enriching the dialogue not only among ourselves as designers, but also with our clients.

When my brother Mike asked us to design the Margarido House in Oakland, California, he and his wife wanted a home that would fulfill the needs of their growing family for years to come. They wanted a home that would inspire them and their children every day, one that would make them conscious of their connection with the natural world rather than their struggle with it. They also wanted their home to be a model of sustainable living for others, inspiring them to educate themselves on the choices they have in creating a healthy home. Parts of the home we created for them appear in the pages of this book, which we believe will help to make sustainable ways of designing and living as commonplace and accessible as they are inspiring.

I look forward to the day when "green" is not the new "black," as it has been so often described lately, but rather the old "blue," tried and true. And *Green Living by Design* will surely serve as a helpful guide to that end. Logically organized and easy to understand, it is an excellent primer on the essentials of living sustainably. We trust the ideas in its pages will open many new "green" doors for the reader, which, once entered, will be impossible to exit.

Timothy McDonald
Principal of Onion Flats/Plumbob, LLC, Architect of Record for the Margarido House in Oakland, the first LEED-H Platinum custom home in Northern California

Creating a
Green Home

There are so many benefits to living in a green home, and more and more Americans are choosing to take advantage of them. Living in a green home is good for your health. It's good for your pocketbook—tax incentives and energy savings can make building and living in a new green home or greening an existing home less costly than building and living in a standard house. And, of course, it's good for the planet. According to a recent study, green homes are expected to make up 10 percent of new home construction by 2010, up from 2 percent in 2005. Consider these specific benefits:

Green Homes Are Healthier

- Natural ventilation as well as the use of mechanical ventilation systems—which bring in and filter fresh air and vent out stale air—keep indoor air clean.

- The use of toxin-free materials and finishes or those with low toxicity limits indoor air pollution, which can be more harmful than outdoor pollution.

- Abundant natural light boosts your mood and is vital to indoor plants, which are natural air detoxifiers.

- Some green materials and home products resist mold and mildew or are antimicrobial.

Green Homes Are Cost Efficient

- On a month-to-month basis, people who live in green homes save money by using less energy and less water than those who live in standard homes.

- A green home can be more durable than most standard homes thanks to high-quality building materials and construction processes, which lead to lower maintenance costs and fewer repairs.

- The value of a green home is often higher than that of a comparable standard home, particularly because the market demand for green homes is on the rise. Some green apartment buildings, for example, bring in rents 10 to 15 percent higher than market rates, and some LEED-certified

Previous page: Rather than razing this house, architect Joseph Eisner adapted it within its original footprint, adding new energy-efficient windows and doors.

Above: Leaving a portion of the roof open on an enclosed terrace surrounded by efficient windows and finished with natural materials literally brings the outdoors in.

homes (*see page 13*) in green developments have outsold the competition 2 to 1.

- Local, state and federal governments as well as utilities are beginning to offer tax breaks and other incentives for building certified green homes or adding green features to your home, as long as they meet accepted green guidelines (of which there are many).

- In the near future, green homes will likely cost less to insure than standard homes. More insurance companies are offering discounts on policies for green homes. By the same token, numerous mortgage companies offer discounted loan rates for homebuyers buying green homes.

Left: High-performance windows and cedar shingles combine character with environmental consciousness.

Above: One approach to creating eco-friendly interiors is to use architectural salvage as art, as designer Janie Hirsch did in this compact home office space.

Green Homes Are Easy on the Earth

- Green homes can use up to 40 less energy than similar standard homes. Some experts suggest that future green homes could even be designed to produce more energy than they consume, through energy harvesting devices such as solar panels or wind turbines.

- Drought-tolerant landscaping, efficient plumbing and bathing fixtures, and water-conservation systems enable green homes to use less water than standard homes.

- Fewer nonrenewable natural resources are used to construct a green home. Many green building materials are made with recycled content. Salvaged materials from demolished buildings are also often used in green homes, as are materials made from rapidly renewable materials, such as bamboo, hemp and soybean-based products. In addition, the use of specially certified woods

helps promote socially and environmentally beneficial forestry practices.

- The construction of a new standard 2,500-square-foot home generates approximately 2 tons of construction waste that typically ends up in landfills. As a result of recycling practices, green home construction reduces waste.

Left: Energy-efficient light fixtures and natural light streaming through ample windows provide eco-friendly illumination in a bathroom designed by architect Joseph Eisner. Above: Natural light flows freely through a staircase, minimizing the need for artificial illumination. Opposite,above: Beautiful, energy-efficient windows add charm and function. Opposite, below: Eco-friendly silk textiles from Lulan enhance a bed with beauty and sustainability.

Incentives Make It Easy to Be Green

Not so long ago, professionals knowledgeable about green design and green building products weren't as commonplace as they are today, so the upfront costs of building a green home were at a premium. But with increasing interest in and growing demand for green design, the cost of owning a green home can be comparable to— or sometimes even cheaper than—owning a standard home, especially when you factor in the upfront green building tax breaks and incentives, and long-term energy savings. For more information on the many local and state governments, utility companies and other entities that offer rebates, tax breaks and other incentives in your area, visit these websites:

- energy.gov/taxbreaks.htm As a result of the Energy Policy Act of 2005, the U.S. government offers various tax breaks and incentives for efficiency upgrades to homes.

- dsireusa.org The Database of State Incentives for Renewables & Efficiency is a nonprofit project funded by the U.S. Department of Energy through the North Carolina Solar Center and the Interstate Renewable Energy Council. It provides information on local, state, federal and utility incentives available for switching to renewable or efficient energy.

- epa.gov/greenbuilding/tools/funding.htm The U.S. Environmental Protection Agency's site offers information on many of the sources of funding for green building available at the national, state and local levels for homeowners, industry, government organizations and nonprofits in the form of grants, tax credits, loans and other sources.

- energystar.gov/taxcredits The U.S. government's site for its Energy Star program provides insight on how consumers, home builders and others can get federal tax credits for using energy-efficient products.

- www.usgbc.org/PublicPolicy/SearchPublicPolicies. aspx?PageID=1776 This link within the U.S. Green Building Council's site will help you find local incentives for building LEED-certified buildings, including homes. (LEED stands for Leadership in Energy and Environmental Design, which was developed by the USGBC and defines criteria for green design. It is generally considered the gold standard by which environmental design is judged.)

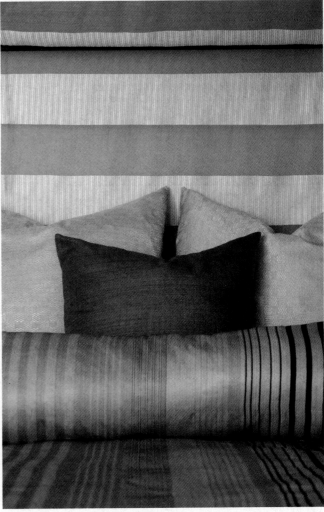

WHAT IS A GREEN HOME?

With increasing public demand for environmentally conscious products, most builders and building product and furniture manufacturers are now cultivating and promoting various green design, production or recycling practices and programs for their goods and services. While there are many different opinions on what constitutes a green home, several national, regional and local green home certification programs exist that help to define minimum green building standards, and most of them aim to accomplish the same essential goals. In general, the guidelines of most building-related organizations and government agencies aim to build new homes that minimize environmental impact by wasting fewer resources during site preparation and construction, recycling and conserving water and materials, reducing carbon buildup, using sustainable and nontoxic materials and finishes whenever possible, ensuring good indoor air quality and creating structures that are at least 15 percent more energy efficient than those built with standard construction practices.

Among the most well-known providers of green building standards are the U.S. Environmental Protection Agency and the U.S. Department of Energy, whose joint Energy Star and WaterSense programs aim to help consumers save money and protect the environment through energy-efficient products and conservation practices. In 2007, the Energy Star program was credited with helping Americans cut the equivalent of 27 million cars worth of greenhouse gas emissions and

Green Guidelines

For more information on various national, regional and local green building programs, visit these sites:

- energystar.gov; epa.gov For information on the federal government's Energy Star and WaterSense programs

- nahb.org For the National Association of Home Builders' green building certification and guidelines for its members

- usgbc.org For the U.S. Green Building Council's Leadership in Energy and Environmental Design (LEED) program's green residential certification standards

- earthcrafthouse.com For the green guidelines of EarthCraft House, a residential green building program of the Greater Atlanta Home Builders Association in partnership with Southface, a nonprofit corporation that provides environmental education and outreach programs

- earthadvantage.com For guidelines from Earth Advantage, a nonprofit organization offering the Northwest region's premier green building program

- builditgreen.org For the guidelines of Build It Green, a nonprofit membership organization that promotes healthy, energy- and resource-efficient building practices in California

- environmentsforliving.com For information on the Environments for Living Certified Green program, developed by the Masco Corporation, one of the world's largest manufacturers of brand-name consumer products for the home. It is a prescriptive program designed to be complementary with "checklist" green building programs, both national and local. The program incorporates the principals of building science.

- eere.energy.gov/buildings/building_america For research conducted by Building America, a private/public partnership sponsored by the U.S. Department of Energy. It conducts systems engineering research to find energy-efficient solutions for new and existing housing constructed on a production basis. Building America unites independent segments of the building industry with teams of architects, engineers, builders, equipment manufacturers, material suppliers, community planners, mortgage lenders and contractors.

- healthhouse.org For guidelines recommended by Health House, a program of the American Lung Association that aims to encourage home construction that meets the most stringent building standards in the U.S. and includes site inspections during construction and performance testing upon completion.

- greenhomeguide.org For information on guidelines for green practices for renovation and remodeling of existing homes developed by the American Society of Interior Designers in partnership with the U.S. Green Building Council. The site also offers information on more than 70 other regional and local green building home programs throughout the U.S.

trim their utility bills about one third, saving them a total of about $16 billion, or $200 to $300 per household. The program awards an Energy Star rating to new homes and appliances that meet strict energy-efficiency guidelines set by the EPA and the DOE. A primary requirement for new homes to earn an Energy Star rating is that they be at least 15 percent more efficient than homes built to the 2004 residential code.

The Energy Star program also includes guidelines for indoor air quality. Homes that receive an Energy Star Indoor Air Package label have met more than 60 requirements for design and construction features that control chemical exposure, radon, moisture, pests and ventilation. The Energy Star ratings systems

A new home designed by architect Joseph Eisner was sited to maximize daylight and conserve energy.

are the most popular in the U.S., with more than 700,000 homes certified since 2003. If you want to make improvements to your home, the EPA also offers tools and resources to help you plan and undertake projects to reduce your energy bills and improve your comfort.

Two other national nonprofit organizations, the National Association of Home Builders and the U.S. Green Building Council, also offer guidelines and certification programs for green design. The NAHB, which claims 235,000 members who are responsible for building about 80 percent of the country's new homes every year, introduced its voluntary Model Green Home Guidelines in 2005. In 2008, it also created a national Green Building Program, which provides three levels of certification and is accredited by the American National Standards Institute. At the same time, it introduced its new Certified Green

Professional educational designation for homebuilders and other industry professionals.

The U.S. Green Building Council, an organization of more than 14,000 companies, public agencies, universities, architects, builders, engineers and environmental groups, is the largest independent organization serving the building industry and is widely regarded as the primary authority on green building and design. Its Leadership in Energy and Environmental Design (LEED) program, long recognized for its green building rating system for commercial architecture, now also offers a rating system for residential green design certification at three different levels: platinum, gold and silver. Officially released at the end of 2007 and known as LEED-H, the USGBC's green home rating system is designed to address single-family and multi-family low-rise homes. For high-rise residential buildings, the system is known as LEED-NC (LEED for new construction), which was introduced in 2000. The systems are similar to that of the NAHB, but more stringent.

Interior doors allow air and natural light to permeate a second-floor room in a home constructed with eco-friendly materials and designed by Wesketch Architecture.

For a new home to get LEED-H certification, 18 prerequisites as well as a minimum number of points from four of eight categories must be met. The eight categories include:

- **Location and linkages** Addresses the environmentally sensitive ways in which a builder chooses a site and promotes responsible land use by limiting infrastructure

elements, such as roads and water and sewage lines, and encouraging transportation options that reduce dependence on automobiles.

- **Sustainable sites** Addresses landscaping and rewards low-maintenance projects with native plants and bioswales or other storm-water runoff techniques.

- **Water Efficiency** Addresses internal and exterior water conservation strategies, and rewards the use of water-efficient fixtures and appliances as well as rainwater harvesting and other measures for irrigation.

Opposite: Certified wood framing, cedar roofing and a mix of eco-friendly siding materials combine curb appeal with sustainability in this home by Wesketch Architecture.

Above: Wood furniture and wall panels made of reclaimed wood give old materials new life in a thoroughly modern setting. Low-VOC stain unifies the wood elements.

A local artisan forged the decorative stair rail of a split-level home that was renovated without recreating the existing structure.

- **Energy and atmosphere** Addresses home energy use and the generation of carbon dioxide, and rewards homes with efficient envelopes and low inherent structural energy use relative to climate zone.

- **Materials and resources** Addresses the choice of building materials, including the environmental impact of harvesting, extracting, transporting and disposing of them. Points are awarded for environmentally conscious materials as well as for reclaimed or recycled-content materials, low-VOC and locally sourced materials, and certified sustainable wood products.

- **Indoor air quality** Addresses the reduction of pollutants that can contaminate the air through the removal of adhesives, finishes and products that emit high levels of volatile organic compounds (VOCs) as well as through the introduction of air filters or fresh-air ventilation systems.

- **Awareness and education** Addresses the encouragement of homeowners to keep abreast of energy consumption and maintenance issues over the lifespan of a home.

- **Innovation and design process** Addresses planning that improves the integration of the systems and elements in a green home as measured against LEED or other regional standards.

How Can You Confirm That Your Home Is Green?

Both the USGBC's LEED and the NAHB's rating systems require an Energy Star certification as a prerequisite to their certification, and so offer higher-level green standards against which a home may be evaluated. The USGBC also offers residential remodeling guidelines for existing homes, known as the ReGreen Guidelines. While these guidelines dovetail with the LEED for Homes Rating System and are intended for professionals, they are not a rating or certification system. They are also accessible to homeowners and do-it-yourselfers.

Among the dozens of other certification programs operated by regional and local home building associations are the Built Green programs in the states of Washington, Colorado, Hawaii and New Mexico, and in Grand Rapids, Michigan, as well as Canada. There are also numerous local electric utilities, local governments and other nonprofit organizations with testing and certification programs.

Inspection and Verification

Most green building rating and certification systems require on-site testing and inspection to confirm that minimum standards are met. With the increase in attention on energy efficiency in our country, hundreds of rating firms have developed in the U.S. over the past couple of decades employing independent evaluators trained in what is known as the Home Energy Rating System, developed by the Residential Energy Services Network (RESNET), a not-for-profit membership corporation and national standards-making body for building energy-efficiency rating systems. Ratings by these certified inspectors can be made for both new and existing homes. In a new home, ratings can verify energy performance for the Energy Star homes program. They can also be used to secure energy-efficient mortgages or verify energy code compliance. If you want to upgrade your home's energy efficiency, you can use the energy rating to pinpoint specific cost-effective improvements. An energy rating can also allow a homebuyer to compare the energy performance of homes under consideration.

A home energy rater reviews such energy characteristics as insulation levels, window efficiency, wall-to-window ratios, heating and cooling system efficiency, orientation of the home in relation to the sun, and the water heating system. The data gathered by the rater is entered into an accredited computer program and translated into what is known as a HERS rating score between 1 and 100, depending on its relative efficiency. The HERS Index score is keyed to a reference based on the International Energy Conservation Code, and each one-point decrease in the score corresponds to a one-point decrease in energy consumption compared to the reference. So the lower a home's HERS Index score, the more energy efficient it is. For example, a home with a HERS Index of 90 is 10 percent more efficient than a home built to meet the standard reference.

Unlike an energy audit or a weatherization assessment, this type of home energy rating is a recognized tool in the mortgage industry. An energy mortgage credits a home's energy efficiency in the home loan. If the home is rated as particularly energy efficient, for example, the rating could give the home buyer the ability to secure an Energy Efficient Mortgage, which uses the energy savings from a new energy-efficient home to increase a consumer's home-buying power and capitalizes the energy savings in the appraisal. For homes in which the energy efficiency can be improved, an Energy

Improvement Mortgage can finance the energy upgrades of an existing home using monthly energy savings. If you plan to purchase a new green home, be sure to enlist some form of independent third-party testing system to verify any green certification claims.

Eco-Smart Elements

A green home may include any number of health-promoting, energy-saving, environment-preserving features. Here are just of the few of the specific elements you might find in a green home:

- Passive energy conservation design features, such as overhangs over south- and west-facing windows
- Well-insulated windows
- A tankless water heater
- Efficient light fixtures and bulbs and glare-free daylighting
- Dual-flush toilets, low-flow faucets, high-efficiency irrigation systems and other water conservation features
- Efficient Energy Star-rated appliances
- Solar-powered energy systems and water heaters
- Countertops or carpets made of recycled materials
- Wood floors or cabinets made from trees grown and harvested in sustainably managed forests
- Efficient air ventilation and purification systems
- Low- or no-VOC paints and finishes
- Fresh-air intakes and fine-particle filters on air conditioners

Groundwork

Whether you rent an apartment, own a condo, live in a home you want to remodel, or plan to buy or build a new home, the best place to start cultivating a greener life is in your own backyard. Before turning your attention inward, get a clear sense of the land your home sits on and the environment that surrounds it, so that you can make your landscape and your neighborhood as eco-friendly as your home.

A good green home minimizes impact on the environment and is as free from hazardous conditions as possible. It is also surrounded by an easy-to-maintain landscape with native plants that promote the health of the local habitat. Ideally, the land around a green home is aesthetically appealing and includes plants that provide shade, absorb carbon and enrich the soil. The landscape might also include retention ponds or bioswales for collecting and filtering storm-water runoff. If you're building a new green home, then you're in the best position to control your immediate environs from the outset by working with your architect and landscaper to develop your site in the most environmentally friendly way. If you live in an existing home on a site that's already developed, however, you can still take steps to better understand your surroundings, remedy problems and nurture earth-friendly conditions in your own yard as well as influence the broader environment around you.

Previous page: The constrained lot of an English-style brick home designed by Wesketch Architecture is enhanced with low-maintenance landscaping. Above: A limited number of plants on an enclosed exterior courtyard keeps water use to a minimum in a home designed by Plumbob, built by McDonald Construction and Development, and named as the first Green Point–rated and LEED-Platinum home in Northern California.

UNDERSTANDING AND INFLUENCING YOUR SURROUNDINGS

One of the best ways to start learning about the environment around your home is to make a map of your surroundings that includes elements such as cell phone towers, industrial smokestacks, high-voltage power lines and landfills that can pose environmental problems. If you live in a city, create a map that covers a five- to 10-block radius; if you live in a suburban or rural area, aim for a two- to five-mile radius for your map.

Note both the manmade features of your neighborhood and environs as well as the natural conditions. Natural conditions you would record on your map might include ponds, lakes, streams, rivers, wildlife preserves, swamps and wetlands. Manmade features might include parks, golf courses, commercial farms and camps, any of which might be sprayed with pesticides or treated with herbicides that can filter into the watershed. Also make note of your neighbors' lawns and landscapes, and record any chemical treatments they might use if you're aware of them, and include high-traffic roads, schools and businesses such as dry cleaners, gas stations, electrical power stations or chemical processing plants that might contribute to the chemical- or electro-pollution in your neighborhood. You should also note the prevailing wind patterns, the position of the sun in relation to the windows in your primary living spaces as well as the location of trees that can provide shade and wind protection for your home.

Once you've gained a clearer sense of the area around your home and have pinpointed the potential problems, you can begin collaborating with neighbors and your community to influence any necessary changes. You might, for example, work with a local school committee to address environmental health concerns for children caused by a school's outdated building materials procurement procedures or ineffective ventilation systems. Or you may join with neighbors to set up a conservation easement to protect a scenic location in your vicinity.

Naturally Occurring Pollutants and Electromagnetic Fields

You would naturally avoid building or buying a home near any business or industrial site that generates excessive manmade pollutants, such as toxic waste, electromagnetic waves, and pesticides, which can cause various kinds of environmental illnesses, including multiple chemical sensitivity and cancer. But there are also natural pollutants, including geopathic stress, electromagnetic radiation, radon and other elements that many environmentalists believe can cause harm to your health and that you should also avoid or control to the best extent possible.

GEOPATHIC STRESS

Naturally occurring earth energies known as geopathic stress come from polar magnetism, veins and streams of water, underground domes, radon gas emissions, electromagnetic waves and seismic activity. They can produce effects such as underground caves, vortices, rock fissures and faults, power spots and other geological stresses. Many of these stresses, such as earthquake fault lines or areas where there are radon gas emissions, for example, are recognized as hazardous, while others, such as naturally occurring noxious geopathic energy lines that crisscross the earth, are more controversial.

Yet some studies have measured significant changes in levels of serotonin, melatonin, calcium and zinc in people living over noxious energy emissions that cause sleep disorders, depression, rapid heart rates and other symptoms. Other studies have shown that plants and animal behavior can indicate areas where geopathic stress occurs. For example, cats, bees and ants are drawn to geopathic stress zones, and oak, elm and willow trees thrive in these areas. Cattle, horses, pigs, sheep, swallows, chickens and dogs, on the other hand, avoid these areas, and fruit trees do not flourish in them. Also, lightning has been reported to be more likely to strike in

Elements of a Green Neighborhood

If you're looking for a neighborhood in which to build a new green home, or if you'd like to get a sense of how your own neighborhood stacks up against others from a green perspective, consider comparing it to measures the U.S. Green Building Council uses to rate the eco-consciousness of communities through its LEED-Neighborhood Development certification rating program. The program identifies several conditions by which the sustainability of a community or neighborhood can be judged. These include:

- A reduction in sprawl development Locations that are closer to existing town and city centers, sites with good access to transit systems, infill or previously developed sites, and sites adjacent to existing developments are preferred. Low-density housing located in automobile-dependent outlying areas can harm the natural environment by consuming and fragmenting farmland, forests and wildlife habitat, degrading water quality through the destruction of wetlands and polluting the air with increased automobile travel.

- An emphasis on healthy living Compact, mixed-use neighborhoods with shops and services within walking or biking distance are preferred. Neighborhoods that promote walking and biking rather than automobile use can improve cardiovascular and respiratory health and reduce the risk of hypertension and obesity in their inhabitants. This approach also addresses what one green home developer calls a "time famine," or lack of time in people's lives, which is one of the biggest driving interests of home buyers. Quick transportation and easy access to recycling centers helps free up more time.

- Land development that protects threatened species Compact development patterns and sites within or adjacent to existing developments that minimize habitat fragmentation and help preserve areas for recreation are preferred.

- Plentiful transportation options that decrease automobile dependence Downtown areas and neighborhood centers that can be accessed easily by buses, trains, car pools, bicycle lanes and sidewalks are preferred.

areas where underground water veins cross and deteriorating or cracking stone or concrete structures can indicate where areas of geopathic stress are present. Studies suggest that these naturally occurring earth energies can become more problematic when they interact with artificially produced electromagnetic fields from underground transportation, sewers, communications systems, computers, appliances, cell phones, wireless technologies and the like.

Some studies have shown that avoiding metal building materials and bed frames, and using wood structural systems and frames instead, can help mitigate the effects of geopathic stress. Experienced dowsers, who practice ancient techniques to understand earth energies, can locate areas of geopathic stress and offer corrective measures.

ELECTROMAGNETIC FIELDS

Some electromagnetic energy waves, such as sunlight, are natural; other fields, such as television and radio waves or microwaves, are not. The magnetic field that envelops the earth is a nonoscillating, direct current at 7.83 cycles per second, similar to that of the human body. It pulses on and off, but always moves in the same direction. Communication in the cells of your body occurs through electrical charges that generate currents that control many of the body's major functions, such as nerve conduction and heartbeat, and these natural fields pulse on and off like that around the earth.

Unlike natural currents, manufactured currents oscillate back and forth in different directions and are known as alternating currents. Many biologists concur that electromagnetic fields have biological effects, but do not agree on the degree to which they are harmful. Studies have indicated, however, that EMFs can contribute to nervous disorders, such as depression and anxiety, and some link exposure to EMFs to elevated child leukemia risks. The long-term consequences of exposure to manufactured radiation are not well understood, though today millions of Americans are in effect participating in an experiment on them. While some countries have set national limits on exposure to certain kinds of electric and magnetic fields, the U.S. has not.

To ensure your property is protected from adverse exposure to manufactured EMFs, some public health experts recommend keeping at least 250 meters from 400 kilovolt lines, 150 meters from 225 kilovolt lines, 100 meters from

63–90 kilovolt lines, and 5 to 10 meters from transformers. Another group of experts—led by David Carpenter, the director of the Institute for Health and the Environment for the State University of New York—reviewed 2,000 studies on EMFs and recommends a 1 milligauss limit for housing adjacent to new or upgraded power lines, a 2 milligauss limit for all other new construction, a 1 milligauss limit for existing housing to project children and pregnant women, and a 0.1 microwatt per square centimeter limit for outdoor cumulative exposure to radio frequencies. You can use a gaussometer to make these calculations.

RADON AND HEAVY METALS
Radon is a radioactive gas formed by the natural radioactive

A pergola, patios and porches enrich the character of a 1950s ranch house renovated by Wesketch Architecture in a Shingle style home without deviating from the contextual scale of the surrounding community.

decay of uranium, which occurs naturally within the Earth's crust, rock, soil and water. Radon is colorless, odorless and tasteless, and can seep from the ground into homes. It can also enter into the groundwater and affect water supplies. Many kits and devices are available to test for radon, which appears at higher levels in some parts of the country more than others. The level at which the EPA recommends action is 4 picocuries. There are a variety of services that can be employed and techniques that can be applied to reduce radon to acceptable levels.

Heavy metals are present in air, food, water and various chemicals, and many of them, such as aluminum, copper and lead, can accumulate in human tissue over time and cause damage to the brain, kidneys and liver. The EPA Consumer Confidence Rule requires that public water suppliers that serve community water systems year-round provide a consumer confidence report (CCR) to their customers. The reports, which are also know as annual water reports or drinking quality reports, summarize the sources used (such as lakes, rivers, aquifers and reservoirs) and any detected contaminants and remedial action or compliance efforts. Water can also become polluted through PVC, lead or copper pipes, or leaks in pipes that permit silt and bacteria to enter the tap water stream. Private well water quality is not governed by EPA regulations, but the standards for public systems are helpful guidelines for the treatment of water from private wells. The EPA recommends testing private water supplies annually for coliform bacteria, nitrates, total dissolved solids and pH levels to detect for water contamination problems regularly.

A 1960s A-frame home was renovated in a Shingle style and fitted with new efficient windows to maximize daylight and minimize environmental impact by preserving the original plan. A new deck links the home to the outdoors.

Site Inspection

Before you make an offer to purchase any property, enlist the help of professional consultants to inspect the property with a Phase I environmental audit, especially if the property has a history of industrial or agricultural use. The cost of an inspection is minor compared to possible hazardous waste cleanup costs. A geotechnical engineer can troubleshoot problems with high water tables, unstable soils, earthquake faults and sink holes. A geotechnical engineer is often also a septic engineer and can perform percolation tests to determine how sewage waste should best be handled and can make recommendations on a proper septic system for the site. If the site lacks water, a water specialist can help you find out the cost of obtaining it, either through the local municipality's water company or by drilling a well, if you must do that. If the property already has a well, its pump should be one that was manufactured after 1979, as oils in older pumps can contain PCBs that can pose a health hazard.

Resources

- **scorecard.org** The website of Environmental Defense, a leading national nonprofit environmental advocacy group, allows you to obtain accessible, scientifically credible information about toxics in your community simply by typing in your zip code. The site also allows you to identify companies with the worst environmental records in your area. By distributing previously inaccessible data, the Scorecard site aims to provide a powerful tool for both citizens and communities to demand improvements in environmental quality.

- **nwf.org** This website offers information on The National Wildlife Federation's Certified Wildlife Habitat program, which helps homeowners turn their backyards into wildlife sanctuaries.

- **susdesign.com/sunangle** This sun angle calculator, offered through the Sustainable by Design website, allows you to find out the position of the sun based on your location, the time and the day of the year.

- **davisnet.com** The website of Davis Instruments, a private manufacturing company and developer of weather-monitoring instruments.

- **weathertrak.com** The website of a water management service and product company.

- **dowsers.org** The website of the American Society of Dowsers, a nonprofit organization that seeks to promote public awareness of the art of dowsing, and to provide and encourage high ethical standards.

- **ewg.org/tapwater/findings.php** The Environmental Working Group's National Tap Water Quality Database enables you to find the CCR for your municipal system.

Left: Linked by a pergola, two cabanas clad in sustainably forested mahogany frame the edge of a pool.

Opposite: Planters made of rusticated, engineered stone form a border at the rear of an eco-friendly house.

Site Clearing and Preparation

Before agreeing to work with a contractor, be sure you clarify and agree upon your demands for minimal impact to the environment. You should be sure that natural vegetation and land features are preserved to the maximum extent possible and that you or your architect will have the authority to approve the site layout before footings are dug. You should also demand that topsoil and boulders be stockpiled, and reserve the right to determine which trees will be removed. Tree stumps should also be removed and disposed of off-site to keep away termites and other pests.

The ground should also be graded to slope at least 5 percent away from the house perimeter for proper water drainage and to prevent mold. And builders should avoid treating soil beneath brick pavers or around the structure with insecticides or pesticides. If soil treatment is required, consider using boric acid on sand surfaces and applying barrier cloth under floors and walkways to prevent weed growth. Finally, avoid using asphalt or blacktop paving, which contains petroleum tar. It is carcinogenic and emits harmful vapors during installation and becomes volatile when heated by the sun. Healthier options include concrete slab, gravel, brick pavers or paving stone.

SHAPING YOUR YARD

The manner in which you maintain your garden or landscape can have a significant effect on your own health and that of the soil, air, water and habitat for native wildlife nearby. If you garden in an environmentally friendly way, using sustainable gardening techniques, you can enhance your environs and help conserve resources. Consider these approaches:

- **Employ passive landscaping techniques.** Plant trees in a way that works with the sun and seasons to improve the heating and cooling of your home. For example, place mature or fast-growing deciduous shade trees near south- and west-facing windows to block high sun from penetrating windows and heating up rooms in summer, while permitting the lower-angle sun to warm rooms in winter after the leaves have fallen. You'll save money on heating and cooling and protect your furnishings and carpets from fading.

- **Restore native plants and remove invasive ones.** Plants native to your region are better for the environment than exotic ones. They generally require less water, fertilizer and other additives, and need less effort in pest control. They are also important to native wildlife, such as pollinators. Pollinators often rely on a certain type of flower as a source of food, and the flower depends on the pollinator to transport its pollen to other flowers to reproduce. Non-native plants can upset the delicate balance of a local ecosystem, sometimes out-competing native species to the point of extinction.

- **Incorporate bioswales.** These or other storm-water systems are designed to remove silt and pollution from surface runoff water. They typically consist of a swaled drainage course with gently sloped sides and are filled with

vegetation, compost or riprap to maximize the time water spends in the swale and trap pollutants and silt. Bioswales and rain gardens are low-impact storm-water systems that can deal with 95 percent of the rainfall onsite as opposed to having it run off the site quickly into pipes channeled into a river or other water feature.

- **Introduce an automatic irrigation system.** Since more water is generally used outside the home than inside, consider integrating an efficient irrigation system into your existing landscape. In new developments, some local homeowners' covenants allow builders to install drip irrigation systems along with drought-tolerant plants and minimal lawns. Also, if you're in the market for a preconstructed green home, look for one in a development that includes water conservation techniques in its building guidelines or certification program. Some communities even mandate WeatherTrak satellite irrigation control. You might also consider purchasing your own electronic or wireless automatic irrigation system, such as Davis's Vantage Pro2, which connects to the company's weather stations around the globe and offers readings for barometric pressure, temperature, humidity, rainfall, wind speed and direction, and much more—without a PC.

- **Harvest rainwater for irrigation.** To do this, you can simply collect rainwater in barrels for your irrigation needs. In a new home, plan for gutters that divert rainwater from the roof into barrels positioned around the side of your

house. In an existing home, you can cut an opening into an existing downspout and divert the water into tanks or barrels. Depending on your location and landscaping needs, you can collect about 375 gallons In a 400-gallon rain barrel from a ½-inch rainfall off one side of a 2,400-square-foot roof. The barrels are about 4 x 4 feet and can be lined up and camouflaged with

shrubs, and the water they hold can be drawn out with a small water pump and used for irrigation during dry summer months.

- **Use mulch.** Mulch helps hold water in the soil, rather than allowing it to evaporate into the air, so it remains available to your plants. Mulching can also help you reduce your watering time. As the mulch breaks down it also provides nutrients to the soil, helping to reduce the need for fertilizer. Use mulches that are derived from sustainable forestry practices and free from pests.

Opposite: A 4,000-gallon rainwater catchment system is buried under the driveway of this home designed by Plumbob and surrounded by drought-tolerant plants.

Left and above: Downspouts at the perimeter of sloped roofs allow runoff water to collect in rain barrels for environmentally sound landscape irrigation.

creating a green home

- **Reduce lawn size.** Grass lawns often require chemical treatments and frequent maintenance with gas-powered lawn mowers, which produce high levels of greenhouse gases that contribute to global warming and air pollution. Most lawns consist of just a few types of plants that most animals do not consume, so they don't provide a lot of value for wildlife either. If you replace grass with native wildflowers, bushes, and trees, you can provide the food, shelter and cover for birds, butterflies and other wildlife that help maintain healthy, natural ecosystems.

- **Try xeriscaping.** Xeriscaping is an approach to landscaping that minimizes outdoor water use and maintains soil integrity with native, drought-tolerant plants. This practice is common in drier areas of the country, such as the West and Southwest, where water is in shorter supply or water quality can be an issue.

- **Create a roof terrace.** If you live in an urban setting and don't have a terrace or ground-level garden, you might still be able to cultivate access to the great outdoors by creating a roof garden. Not only will it improve the quality of your life, but it will also increase the value of your home, as a potential buyer will pay a premium for garden space in urban areas.

Opposite: Sedum, planted in gravel-filled trays, covers part of the rooftop garden of architect Rick Renner's urban apartment. The plants help with insulation and rooftop runoff.

Above: Designer Brian Flynn designed this stylish, low-maintenance rooftop garden, adding value to his Atlanta apartment and giving him access to the outdoors.

Simple Steps to Turn Your Home into an Eco-Friendly Sanctuary

1 Use solar garden lights to line pathways. These fixtures do not require wiring or electricity. Instead they absorb natural sunlight during the day and turn on automatically at dusk. Some use LED (light-emitting diode) bulbs, which are brighter and last longer than standard incandescent bulbs.

2 Put out a birdbath or bird feeder. The birds that come to indulge in them will introduce movement, color and song to your yard—and they'll eat up many harmful insects, too. Use platform feeders to attract blue jays, cardinals, robins and sparrows; hanging feeders for goldfinches, purple finches and various chickadees; pole feeders for certain woodpeckers or mockingbirds. Use a brightly colored hummingbird feeder to attract hummingbirds and use suet feeders to attract insect-eating birds, such as thrush and tanagers.

3 Build a bat house. As eerie as they are to many people, bats are actually environmentally helpful friends. They eat thousands of mosquitoes in a single evening and they also eat cockroaches and gnats. In addition to their pest control abilities, they pollinate many food plants.

4 Attract butterflies. Plant buddleia, aster, goldenrod, clover, hyacinth and other plants that butterflies love. You'll enrich your garden with the color and movement of these beautiful creatures and help pollinate plants. Just be sure they're in a sunny, warm, relatively wind-free place with access to water, and choose plants that are attractive to the butterflies in your area. Don't use pesticides on such plants.

5 Deer-proof your yard. Include plants deer tend to avoid, such as marigolds and zinnias, or place scented soap or human hair in your gardens. Another option is to use very tall fences or netting fences.

6 Protect your pets. Keep plants that may be delightful to humans but toxic to your pets out of your garden. Visit the toxic plant database at the website of the University of Illinois's Library of Veterinary Medicine at *library.uiuc.edu/ vex/toxic/comlist.htm.*

Above: Surrounded by a deck of durable Western Red Cedar, a 12-inch-deep garden insulates this home designed by Plumbob, and controls storm water.

Left and opposite: EcoSource's 100 percent biodegradable greenPots and low-maintenance plants enrich a home's surroundings without harming the planet.

Creating an
Efficient,
Eco-Friendly
Building
Structure

STARTING FRESH OR STARTING FROM SCRATCH

Whether you want to remodel an existing home to make it greener or build or purchase a new green home, it is essential to understand the characteristics of the home's building envelope. The envelope of a green home should be tight and energy efficient with well-insulated walls, efficient windows, and effective vapor and ventilation control.

A major problem with many existing and new homes built with standard frame construction, for example, is the location and handling of the mechanical equipment. Furnaces, boilers and air handlers should not be placed in vented crawl spaces or in attics that are not properly insulated. Vents in attics and crawl spaces, as well as openings for plumbing and wiring, allow air leakage that can cause a home to lose up to 30 percent of its energy. Other energy inefficiencies result from poor construction or design, such as improperly placed roof sheathing or interior drywall that isn't tight at key connection points inside the house, such as next to a kitchen cabinet or bathtub adjoining a home's perimeter wall. Poor exhaust fans in bathrooms can also cause moisture-related problems with mold and mildew that create indoor air quality issues.

It's a real headache to rip out and repair structural problems or inefficient building envelopes. But if you're planning to remodel or want to improve the energy efficiency of your existing home's envelope, it's helpful to get a building inspection to examine the attic, ducts and exhaust vents, and get a RESNET blower door and duct pressurization test done to see if your home meets minimum standards of air tightness. This will help you determine where any problems might be, so that upgrades can be made accordingly.

If you're in the market to buy a preconstructed green home, there are numerous green developments and communities throughout the country. A good way to find one is to review the list of builders in your area who are participating in the government's Energy Star program. Its website enables you to search for builders by state. If you want to build a new green home or remodel an existing home using green principles, be sure to find an architect, builder or other industry professionals who have the knowledge and experience to cost-effectively plan, design and build a green home.

Finding an Architect or Builder

One source for finding design and construction professionals is the U.S. Green Building Council. There are many architects, designers and other professionals who have experience in green design and building, but who are not certified by the Council, however. Local chapters of the American Institute of Architects or the American Society of Interior Designers

Resources for Green Builders, Architects and Designers

- energystar.gov/homes The website for the U.S. Government's energy efficiency rating program.
- www.usgbc.org/DisplayPage.aspx?CategoryID=1306 The U.S. Green Building Council's professional resource link.
- aia.org The site for the American Institute of Architects, which allows you to find architects in your area who specialize in sustainable design. Alternatively, you might contact the state or local chapter of the AIA in your area for recommendations.
- bau-biologieusa.com/findexpert.html The International Institute for Bau-Biologie & Ecology, a nonprofit organization dedicated to education on environmentally healthy building and design, which should be able to refer you to experts familiar with its principles.
- asid.org The site for the American Society of Interior Designers, which allows you to locate interior designers specializing in sustainable design.
- greenbuilding.com A thorough source for finding experts, contractors, builders and green building information.

should also be able to help refer you to green architects in your area. The American Society of Interior Designers can help you locate interior designers who specialize in green design. Another source for finding professionals committed to sustainable design is the International Institute for Bau-Biologie and Ecology. It is a nonprofit educational organization offering information on an integrated sustainable approach to building design, which was developed in Germany and brings together technical expertise, biology and ecology to create healthy homes and workplaces.

Previous page: Two bump-outs clad in stucco and painted to match existing wood siding below increase the area on a home's second floor without altering its original footprint.

Above: This deck is made of Blue Star Mahogany, which is harvested from managed forests independently certified by the Malaysian Timber Certification Council.

creating an efficient, eco-friendly building structure   41

EARTH MASONRY AND OTHER ALTERNATIVE GREEN CONSTRUCTION METHODS

Building a new green home affords you the opportunity to create a dwelling that is sited to work in tandem with the natural cycles of the earth and constructed of the most healthy, locally produced and efficient materials available. Ideally, your architect will also employ a climate-based approach to its construction detailing.

Historically, building types emerged over time that incorporated local materials that responded perfectly to their climactic conditions. Since World War II, however, with the introduction of mass-produced and transported building products, the building industry has changed dramatically. Furthermore, the codes that regulate the building industry do not always address variations in climactic conditions in different parts of the country. With increased dependence on mechanized heating and cooling systems and tighter insulated building envelopes, most houses in the U.S. are now constructed in a similar manner and don't necessarily take into account the extreme weather conditions that have begun to occur due to global warming.

Because of these environmental drawbacks to standard frame construction, some sustainable architects prefer using historical methods of construction and natural materials. The reason why earth masonry and other so-called indigenous modes of earth construction are appealing is that they typically produce massive walls that are designed to handle the transfer of moisture and vapor into and out of the house in a stable, healthy and comfortable way, without the need for manufactured exterior sheathing, insulation, gypsum board and paint, which can cause VOC contamination. Other benefits of earth as a building material are its low cost, recyclability, nonflammability, durability and excellent thermal storage characteristics.

A downside of these construction methods is that the building technique itself can dictate the aesthetic qualities of the home, which may not coincide with your vision. Also, some jurisdictions do not permit earth-masonry or some of the other alternative building approaches, or the methods simply aren't practical or desired. Furthermore, finding contemporary builders familiar with these construction methods can be a challenge.

If you choose to use an earth or other historic green construction method, however, and have an architect and builder who are experienced with it, then you'll also need to get approval to build in this manner from your local building authority, as codes for these construction methods vary by jurisdiction. Here is a brief summary of some options:

- **Earth Block** Used throughout the world in hot, dry subtropical areas, earth blocks can be made in the form of adobes, pressed blocks or green bricks. Its R-value, or insulation capability, is fairly low, so it typically needs to be paired with synthetic insulation to meet energy requirements in the U.S. It is commonly used in the Southwest.

- **Rammed Earth** Historically found in both hot, dry areas and cold, wet regions, rammed-earth structures are made of sand, gravel, clay and moisture that's been rammed into formwork in 6- to 8-inch layers. With modern energy requirements, this type of construction is most suited to warmer climates, but has been adapted to include an insulation layer for colder climates. It has also been produced efficiently with modern mechanized machinery.

- **Cob and Wet Clay Techniques** Cob construction involves the use of moistened clay and sand mixed with straw and then formed into loaves, which are piled onto a wall and blended with previous layers. It's also best suited to warmer climates. An American company, the Cob Cottage Company, has developed a controlled, stronger formulation to create new homes using this process.

- **Light Clay-Straw** In colder climates where higher insulation values are required, mud mixed with lightweight aggregates, such as straw, wood chips, pumice or vermiculite, can serve as a suitable earth-friendly construction material. The EcoNest Building Company has developed a technique for building clay-straw structures in the U.S. that involves applying a clay-straw mixture around a timber frame or as an infill material. Proper curing is essential for this material, and the walls must be finished with earth and lime plaster or properly vented wood siding for sufficient vapor diffusion.

- **Straw Bale** This type of construction is credited to early settlers of the Nebraskan plains, where few trees made wood building supplies scarce but straw was plentiful. Its high insulation value (between R-33 and R-57) makes it a good building material in colder climates. If you want to work with this type of construction, choose straw that has been organically grown to avoid the toxic affects of pesticides. Also, cellulose material is predisposed to mold, so strict moisture and ventilation strategies need to be included in the design with earth-based plaster covering exterior and interior walls. Usually, straw bale construction is combined with various structural systems, such as posts and beams or masonry concrete piers.

- **Wood Insulated Concrete Forms** Invented in Europe after World War II, wood insulated concrete forms (WICFs) were developed to address the massive rebuilding needed during a conventional building material shortage. The units are made of waste wood chips impregnated with clay and mixed with cement. They are lightweight, noncombustible, dimensionally stable, resist rot and fungus, and tolerate freeze-thaw cycles. These vapor-diffusible building components can be combined with insulation inserts to produce economical and energy-efficient structures. Look for the forms that are made without polystyrene. They're available in this country through Durisol, Faswall and Healthy Buildings Made Easy.

- **Aerated Autoclaved Concrete** Manufactured in America by Aercon, Contec, Tru-Stone and Humabuilt HumaBlock, aerated autoclaved concrete (AAC) was developed in Sweden in the 1920s. Since refined, it's a concrete block-like material made from quartz sand, lime, or cement aluminum powder and water. It's highly insulative, and can be reinforced, cut, sawed, shaped and plastered with no toxic outgassing.

- **Structural Insulated Panel (SIP)** is another new composite home building material. These high-performance building panels are typically made by sandwiching a core of rigid foam plastic insulation between two structural skins of oriented strand board (OSB). The building system is extremely strong, energy efficient and cost effective, saving time, money and labor in the building process. SIP homes go up faster than traditionally framed buildings. Panels can be manufactured as big as 8 x 24 ft, so entire walls can be put up quickly, reducing dry-in time. SIPs can be supplied as ready-to-install building components when they arrive at the jobsite, eliminating the time needed to perform individual jobsite operations of framing, insulating and sheathing stick-framed walls. Window openings may be precut in the panels, and depending on the size, a separate header may not need to be installed. Electrical chases are typically provided in the core of the panels, so there is no need to drill through studs for wiring. They were formally accepted into the International Residential Code by the International Code Council in May 2007, and when combined with other energy-efficient systems, can offer 50 to 70 percent savings over the Model Energy Code (MEC). They have also been instrumental in creating what are known as zero-energy buildings, which actually produce more energy than they consume.

Since there are many ways to evaluate and certify a green home, and many building products are now made with at least some kind of eco-conscious production process, you can certainly build a new green home or remodel an existing one using a contemporary standard construction method. Most new homes today are built using metal or wood frame construction methods, and code-approved, mass-produced building materials in uniform sizes with predictable performance characteristics. If you choose to buy or build a new green home that has a standard frame construction, the key is to create an energy-efficient building envelope with high R-value walls by incorporating good insulation, efficient windows, vapor control layers and ductwork in unvented spaces.

Green Certification Organizations

Windows, doors and other exterior building products with seals of approval from any of the following organizations and programs will be certified for various aspects of environmental sensitivity.

- **Forest Stewardship Council** This organization was founded to coordinate the development of forest management standards throughout the U.S. and is the most widely respected certifying body of green wood products of all kinds. Visit *fscus.org*.

- **Sustainable Forestry Initiative** SFI Inc. is a fully independent charitable organization dedicated to promoting sustainable forest management. Paper or wood products with its label have met its standards for environmental responsibility. Visit *sfiprogram.org*.

- **Alliance to Save Energy** Made up of members of Congress and corporate executives, this organization is committed to promoting energy efficiency. Visit *ase.org*.

- **Energy Star** The U.S. government's energy performance rating program. Visit *energystar.gov*.

- **Green Seal** An independent nonprofit organization that strives to achieve a healthier and cleaner environment by identifying, certifying and promoting green products and services. Window and door products that are Green Seal certified meet the organization's energy efficiency requirements and are manufactured and packaged in a consistent, environmentally responsible manner. Visit *greenseal.org*.

- **Metafore** Formerly the Certified Forest Products Council, this nonprofit organization collaborates with businesses and society to create market-based approaches to support forests and communities. Visit *metafore.org*.

- **The National Fenestration Rating Council** The NFRC is a voluntary third-party certification program designed to ensure accurate window performance rating and labeling. Visit *nfrc.org*.

In addition to using local building materials in harmony with your climate, your architect or builder should try to use nontoxic materials whenever possible on the exterior of the house as well as inside. For the concrete used for footings, foundation walls or slab flooring, for example, you might try to get your builder to substitute magnesium oxide–based cement for Portland cement. Although research has been done and efforts have been made to improve it from a green perspective, Portland cement has been estimated to contribute to as much as 12 percent of the earth's greenhouse gas emissions, and when mixed with plastics, it may not cure properly and outgases toxic fumes. It is also susceptible to mold. In addition, any concrete in your home should be made with potable-quality water and clean natural mineral aggregates, not crushed brick, sandstone or cinder. If the concrete needs to be reinforced, it's best to use nonmetallic reinforcing fibers rather than metal wire fabric, or fiberglass bars rather than steel bars to reduce the amount of conductive metals in the house.

In general, for new construction or renovation projects, urge your architect or builder to avoid or limit the use of the following: products that have been treated with insecticides, mildewcides or other chemical treatments; composite wood products bound with formaldehyde-emitting glues, including particleboard; certain kinds of plywood and manufactured sheathing; finishes that emit harmful VOCs; and asphalt roofing materials and driveways. If earth-friendly substitutes cannot be made for these building products, efforts should be made to reduce their effects, such as curing or sealing them off-site.

Framing, Sheathing and Insulation

Like earth masonry and other historic green building methods, the green characteristics of a home built with standard frame construction need to be evaluated for their durability, thermal and moisture control characteristics, and the toxicity of their materials. Here is a summary of some of the primary components of a house built with frame construction and some green approaches to employ:

- **Framing** Frame construction, which is standard in this country since lumber is plentiful, is typically done with 2 x 4 lumber. Metal studs are generally used in urban settings for fire safety. If you opt to build or remodel a house with

this type of construction, you can use framing lumber that has been sustainably harvested, often at no additional cost, if your architect or builder specifies it. Finger-jointed studs made from reclaimed wood scraps offer another framing alternative. They measure 2 x 6 and their increased width allows for more insulation, making a home more energy efficient in climates where extra insulation is helpful.

Opposite and above: Natural materials add character to two homes designed by Wesketch Architecture. An eyebrow arch clad in cedar shingles enlivens the front entrance of a renovated split-level home (*opposite*). Durable slate shingles cover the roof of a new home (*above*) designed and constructed to follow the natural topography of the site.

- **Sheathing** Like framing lumber, exterior-grade plywood sheathing for walls and roofs should be specified to be certified as sustainably harvested. Plywood sheathing as well as another common sheathing material known as oriented strand board (OSB) can contain formaldehyde and other toxic chemicals.

- **Insulation** Any insulation can be seen as a green choice because it improves a home's energy efficiency. But there are many types of insulation, and some are greener than others. To understand the green characteristics of any insulation, you'll want to consider the resources and manufacturing processes used in its production, as well as

its durability, recyclability and impact on indoor air quality. Several green resources, including GreenBuilding.com and TreeHugger.com, evaluate these characteristics.

These websites are also good resources for information on new green insulation alternatives to standard fiberglass insulation, which, although widely used in homes in the U.S., can release particulate matter and harmful gases into the air. Some of the greener alternatives include insulation made from soybeans, cotton, recycled paper, used denim

Wesketch Architecture added smaller north-facing windows to permit views and higher south-facing windows to let in an abundance of natural light.

Types of Insulation

Before choosing any insulation, familiarize yourself with the four types of insulation and their R-values.

Batt and blanket insulation This is the most common form of insulation and usually consists of mineral fiber, either fiberglass or rock wool. It's fairly easy to work with and is generally the least expensive. However, it doesn't seal air as well as other types. It's used to insulate below floors, above ceilings and within walls, and is best suited for standard stud and joist spacing that is mostly free of obstructions.

Loose-fill insulation Loose fibers of rock wool, fiberglass or cellulose can be blown into building cavities or attics using special equipment. It costs more than batts, but reduces air leakage in wall cavities if it is blown in with sufficient density, and has better sound reduction qualities. Cellulose fiber, made from recycled newspapers, is chemically treated for fire and insect resistance. It can be used in walls, floors or attics and you can install it yourself.

Rigid board insulation Made from fiberglass, polystyrene and polyurethane, rigid insulation is used for reroofing work on flat roofs, on basement walls, as perimeter insulation at concrete slab edges, and in cathedral ceilings. If you use it inside, it must be covered with 12-inch gypsum board or other building-code-approved material for fire safety. If used to insulate the interior of masonry walls, it does not require extra vapor-retarding treatment. Exterior applications, however, must be covered with weatherproof facing.

Spray foam Spray foam insulation is a two-part liquid containing a polymer, such as polyurethane or modified urethane, and a foaming agent. It expands into a solid cellular plastic that fills every nook and cranny. Materials and installation, which should only be done by professionals, cost more than traditional batt insulation. However, spray foam acts as both insulation and an air barrier, so it eliminates the usual steps necessary to ensure air-tightness, such as caulking, applying house wrap and vapor barriers, and taping joints. This can make spray foam cost-competitive with batt insulation. Spray foam in small containers may be appropriate when replacing windows or doors.

and even hemp. Bio-based spray foam insulation is said to contain no harmful or irritating microfibers or organic dust particles. The continuous air barrier that it creates around the home not only insulates but also blocks harmful

outside irritants such as mold, pollen and other allergens from entering the home. Another source for information on the various types of insulations and the recommended R-values for your area is the U.S. Department of Energy's Consumer Guide to Energy Efficiency and Renewable Energy (see Guidance sidebar, page 46).

If you're remodeling a kitchen or bathroom, naturally you'll be concerned with the aesthetics, but if you are ripping out drywall anyway, take the opportunity to add insulation, which not only improves energy efficiency but also reduces noise and increases fire resistance. Sources of less harmful batt insulation include CertainTeed and Knauf Fiber Glass, whose insulation is certified by Greenguard, an organization dedicated to improving indoor air quality.

Thermal and Moisture Control

In addition to the thermal control provided by insulation, houses with frame construction also need moisture control and internal air barriers that prevent mold and other moisture damage and block the fumes of unhealthy building materials.

There are four basic approaches to water penetration control in buildings:

- **Mass** This involves traditional, solid structures, including solid concrete, masonry and timber structures, which shed most surface water, effectively absorb the remainder, and subsequently release absorbed moisture as a vapor.

- **Barrier** These structures are designed to completely shed surface water with no moisture penetration and include exterior insulation finish systems (EIFS) and stucco or clapboard walls built without a drainage plane.

- **Internal drainage plane** Structures using this approach include typical stucco and clapboard walls built with a drainage plane or moisture barrier located between the exterior cladding and the supporting wall that provides extra moisture resistance.

- **Rain screen** This approach, which can be applied to brick veneer cavity walls, furred-out clapboard walls, and drainable EIFS, involves a moisture-management system incorporating the exterior cladding, air cavity, drainage plane and airtight support wall to offer a variety of moisture-shedding pathways. There are two types of rain screens: simple rain screens and pressure-equalized rain screens (PERs).

How to Find Eco-Friendly Exterior Products

For more information on green exterior product choices, visit these sites:

- greendepot.com An online green building products retailer for homeowners and professionals. The site's trained staff will also offer product guidance.

- buildinggreen.com A membership-based e-commerce and information site for professionals.

- igreenbuild.com Offers insight and expert tips in LEED certification, sustainable design, energy conservation, green building materials and hundreds of other categories.

- treehugger.com See its Design + Architecture section for information on new green products for the home.

- lowimpactliving.com Online source for all kinds of green products.

- builditgreen.org A professional nonprofit membership organization whose mission is to promote healthy, energy- and resource-efficient buildings in California.

Simple rain screens are effective in climates with an annual precipitation of less than 60 inches; PERs are effective in climates with an annual precipitation of 60 inches or more.

The approach your architect and builder uses will depend on the style of your home and the level of rainfall in your area.

For a house with a frame construction, special foundation detailing with integrated flashing systems and layers of material membranes will provide various levels of damp-proofing, vapor control and soil gas control, including low-emission products to block the entry of radon, if that's an issue in your area. As buildings become tighter and better insulated, the transfer of water vapor through the building shell has become more problematic. With the addition of thermal insulation in the cavity walls of houses built with frame construction, moisture can become trapped in the insulation, rather than flow through the wall to evaporate and dry out, and can therefore result in mold and rot that can damage the assembly. To avoid these conditions, your architect and builder should be able to offer green options for various sealants, membranes and roof underlayments to protect the structure of your home. Tyvek housewrap is one common vapor retardant, for example. They should also be able to recommend site- and climate-based design strategies that can mitigate or control potential problems.

If you're remodeling a home and open your walls to find moisture problems such as rot and mold, do not attempt to clean or repair the problem yourself, as certain types of mold are extremely harmful. Contact a professional inspector with experience in indoor air-quality issues.

Guidance on Creating an Energy-Efficient Envelope

For more information on comparisons among the different kinds of insulation and weatherproofing, visit these sites:

- energystar.gov Offers information on energy-efficient windows and doors, and a Thermal Bypass Inspection Checklist provides valuable guidance on all the steps needed to ensure proper installation. Visit the "Air Seal and Insulation" section of the site for more information on installation techniques.

- toolbase.org For a more detailed description of various insulation types.

- greenguide.com For information on insulation and other green issues.

- eere.energy.gov/consumer The U.S. Department of Energy's Energy Efficiency and Renewable Energy site for consumers offers insight on many home energy–related concerns.

- pathnet.org A voluntary partnership between leaders of the homebuilding, product manufacturing, insurance, and financial industries and representatives of federal agencies, The Partnership for Advancing Technology in Housing offers some simple guidance on choosing the right insulation for the job, including some popular green alternatives.

- naima.org The North American Insulation Manufacturers Association: an industry trade group that offers insight on insulation alternatives. Or look at its consumer site: *simplyinsulate.com*.

- eeba.org The Energy & Environmental Building Association offers climate-based moisture-control strategies.

Exterior Cladding

The exterior cladding you use on your home is key to its character and its curb appeal. Its aesthetic qualities should harmonize with its environs, but it should also be suited to your lifestyle and climate. Even the microclimate of your site should be taken into account to avoid a siding failure. From a green perspective, a siding material should be judged on its abundance and accessibility in your area as well as its sustainability, durability and lack of toxicity. Here is a brief summary of siding options and their attributes, green or otherwise.

- **Brick** In most houses, brick is used as a siding material on a wood frame structure rather than a structural material itself. Good-quality brick is a sustainable choice that will withstand most of the forces that deteriorate other siding products. Maintenance applies mostly to the mortar used to hold the bricks together, while newer mortar material may not require tuck pointing restoration as often, it may require moss control, water sealing and the correction of any deteriorating bricks or settling cracks.

Sustainable brick was used as a siding material on this wood frame structure, designed by Wesketch Architecture to resemble an English-style cottage.

• **Wood siding** There are many varieties of wood siding, from cedar shingles, traditional bevel cedar siding, plywood products and vertical cedar siding to various forms of premanufactured wood siding, such as hardboards, oriented strand board, plywood and masonites. Good-quality wood siding is a good green choice in many areas and, when properly maintained, can remain in excellent condition for years. Wood siding, like all other products, needs to be properly installed, however. But unlike many other siding products, it can be fairly easily repaired or replaced.

Not all wood siding products are of equal quality. Thin, bevel, tight-knot siding products, for example, are typically manufactured from young trees, which do not have good dimensional stability, making them prone to shrinkage, warping and splitting. And unlike old growth cedar, they do not resist rot well. When cedar shingles are used as a sidewall product, a good quality paint, stain or sealer should be used to minimize splitting and warping. Improper installation of siding over the vapor barrier and insulation can result in a higher humidity content in the siding, and eventually add to paint and moisture-related deterioration problems.

Above and opposite, top left: Natural shingle siding gives two renovated homes timeless appeal. Porticos, with their classic columns, along the facade add timeless style to one house (*above*). The other home (*opposite*) was a split-level dwelling constructed after World War II. New intersecting Dutch gables give it a new sense of order and character.

Opposite, top right: Developed in 1895, low-maintenance bark shingles, now available from *barkhouse.com*, require no sealers, stains or paint and can last up to 80 years.

Opposite, below: The metal roof/siding of this house is reflective and dramatically reduces the cost of cooling its interior spaces during the summer months.

- **Aluminum siding** This is a relatively low-maintenance product over the first years of its life, but it is subject to dents and blemishes. It also requires careful washing and eventually repainting. Because metal is conductive, it's not a preferred green product. A painting job on aluminum siding must be carefully prepared, using a primer specifically selected for the siding. A good craftsman can replace individual pieces with matching siding as needed, but since certain patterns of aluminum siding are often discontinued, be sure to stock up on a few extra pieces of your pattern for future replacement if you choose this material.

- **Vinyl siding** This product is made of polyvinyl chloride, which produces potentially serious toxicity problems during manufacture and disposal. However, it does not rot or peel and it can work quite well in many standard home designs, though it requires careful installation or water can wick up behind the siding and rot the sheathing wall behind it. Also, the siding must be protected by a good roof overhang and must be washed from time to time. Heat from outdoor grills can melt and burn it, and difficulty finding matching replacement pieces can make it very hard to repair. From a green perspective, vinyl siding is not a particularly popular option.

- **Stucco** Often installed on masonry or adobe structures, stucco is a very common siding material in areas with a

Mediterranean, or relatively dry, climate. Made of sand, lime and cement, it isn't recommended in wet climates. Stucco on older wood frame homes was often applied over a wood lath, which can deteriorate over time and crack and separate from the wall structure, resulting in moss and mildew growth, paint blistering and noticeable repair patches.

- **Exterior Insulation Finish Systems (EIFS)** EIFS siding involves the application of a plasticized cement stucco product over an exterior-mounted polystyrene foam board insulation, usually top-coated with an acrylic polymer sealant. The system promises low cost, ease of application and a clean look. But moisture can be trapped behind the siding and cause wood rot and other damage, prompting a number of jurisdictions to ban EIFS siding. According to some industry reports, the failure rate of EIFS siding is higher than that of any other siding system on the market, and some insurance companies are reportedly refusing to insure homes and buildings with this type of siding. To solve some of the problems associated with EIFS siding, various water management solutions involving more complicated flashing and caulking systems provide for a secondary shield behind the EIFS siding and for a way to drain any water that penetrates the primary water barrier.

- **Panelized shingle siding systems** This type of siding consists of short panels with one or more rows of thin shingles, which are laminated onto a plywood-like base. The factory-fabricated panels are low-cost and can be quickly installed at the building site, but the thin shingle surfaces are more prone to weather damage, and the panels tend to expand and bulge. Panelized shingle siding seems to perform quite well on exterior surfaces that are protected, properly installed, primed and painted. The best kind of panelized siding uses a thicker shingle (½" or so at the bottom edge).

- **Manufactured siding and lap siding (LP)** Siding manufactured from oriented strand board and other wood composites has the advantage of being manufactured from relatively low-cost wood and young trees, thus saving money and attempting at a more benign impact on the environment, but reports indicate that many of these products have experienced moisture-related problems often related to its installation requirements. However, they are durable and the range in styles is diverse—you can get stucco panel, reverse board and batten, colonial beaded lap, and even stainable shakes. And they're usually treated to help resist fungal decay and termites.

- **Hardi Board and Hardi Plank Siding** These newer products are concrete composites and look like bevel or lap siding, and the reports on them are promising.

Roofing

On a green home, a well-sloped roof with a considerable overhang is generally preferred to a flat or low-sloped roof. Sloped roofs shed water quickly, and overhangs, which can be sized to suit the solar conditions in your area, provide shade in summer and permit solar heat entry in winter. They also protect the walls and foundation from water damage by directing water away from the structure. Water can puddle on flat roofs, which have a higher failure rate, and lead to moisture-related problems.

How to Find Eco-Friendly Exterior Products

For more information on Green exterior product choices, visit these sites:

- Greendepot.com: An online green building products retailer for homeowners and professionals. The site's trained staff will also offer product guidance.

- Building Green.com: A membership-based e-commerce and information site for professionals.

- igreenbuild.com: Offers insight and expert tips in LEED certification, sustainable design, energy conservation, green building materials and hundreds of other categories.

- TreeHugger.com: See its Design + Architecture section for information on new green products for the home.

- Lowimpactliving.com: Online source for all kinds of green products.

- Builtitgreen.com: A professional non-profit membership organization whose mission is to promote healthy, energy and resource-efficient buildings in California.

Wesketch Architecture combined the latest building technology with hand-split roof cedar shakes, reclaimed hand-cut cedar logs, and solid cedar beams and trusswork to sensitively remodel a carriage house on a stone foundation designed almost 90 years ago by architect George Post.

Not so long ago, roof choices were limited mostly to shingles, shakes and composition roofing. Metal roofs on residential construction were rare and ceramic tile roofs were used mostly in the Southwestern states in this country. Today, dozens of roofing products on the market make the choice a little more difficult.

Many of the new roofing products are being developed in response to the shortcomings of older roofing materials, the demands of modern building techniques, and ever more stringent building codes. For example, most of today's building materials are tested and rated for their fire resistance and flame spread. Similarly, most roofing materials are covered by a manufacturer's warranty, with typical warranties ranging from 20 to 40 years. Cost alone does not determine quality, which is good news, since roof replacement is one of the most expensive aspects of the typical home's construction and maintenance program. This brief summary of common roofing options can help you home in on the best choice for you.

- **Asphalt shingles** Also known as composition shingles, they are used on almost 80 percent of North American homes, and are popular due to their durability, reasonable price and ease of maintenance. Asphalt shingles have either a fiberglass mat base or a composition base of organic felt, which is a blend of paper and wood fibers. In either case, the base material is soaked in an asphalt compound with embedded mineral granules. These shingles include a vast

array of colors, profiles and textures. Special chemicals are also blended into the shingles to make them mold- and algae-resistant. Sun and rain can cause asphalt shingles to crack. Because these shingles outgas when heated by the sun, however, green designers prefer to avoid them.

- **Metal** This roofing material is highly reflective and emissive, creating what is known as a cool roof, meaning it can reduce cooling loads by 20 percent or more and help cool urban heat islands. Metal roofing can be made with recycled materials and is recyclable at the end of its life cycle. It is a good choice for flat or low-slope roofs (roofs with slopes

from ¼ to 3 inches per foot). It is also ideal in forested, moss-prone or rainy areas. Typically manufactured from steel, aluminum or copper, it is lightweight, durable, fire-retardant and almost maintenance-free. The cost of metal roofing is initially higher than that of composition shingles, but it has a longer life cycle and reduces energy costs.

- **Clay and concrete tiles** These roofing elements can be ceramic (e.g., clay fired at a high temperature) or fabricated from cement concrete. They can withstand harsh elements, such as hail, wind and fire, and they last a long time: their minimum duration is 50 years. Roofing tiles are available in a wide range of colors. Though more data on their solar reflectance properties is needed, a good starting point to use for estimating their reflectance would be the reflectance of a paint coating of similar color. Tile won't rot or burn and can't be harmed by insects. It is also energy efficient and fire resistant. Tile roofs often have enhanced air circulation compared to other roofing types because ambient air can circulate below as well as above the tile. But they are very heavy and require certain structural standards for the frame and roof decking. Tiles are also fragile and rather costly.

- **Wood shingles** If rot-resistant woods, such as cedar, are used, this roofing material can be good in areas where fire danger is low and humidity is moderate. Wood roofs should also have a provision for air circulation below them

Roofing and Siding Information and Advice

For more information on the selection or removal of roofing and siding, contact these sources:

- builditgreen.org Offers a wide range of information on various siding and roofing options.

- Your local Air Pollution Control Agency For more information about cement asbestos siding, asbestos abatement, and guidelines for homeowners who wish to undertake the removal of cement asbestos siding themselves.

- (800) 898-2842 (NAHB) or (800) 294-EIMA (the EIFS trade association) For the industry point of view on EIFS.

- Your local Household Hazardous Waste Information Hotline For information on how to dispose of leftover paints and other household products in accordance with the law.

- metalroofing.com and themetalinitiative.com For information on cool-roof options.

- Your state Department of Labor and Industries, Office of Health and Safety For information on how to address concerns related to homes painted with older exterior paint products that often contain high levels of lead. Paint chips and sanding dust from such buildings can be ingested or inhaled by small children or can contaminate the soil.

- paintquality.com The Rohm and Haas Paint Quality Institute's site for paint tips and information.

to make sure they always remain dry. This enhanced air circulation helps the roof shed solar heat more readily. They are beautiful, but require careful workmanship and high maintenance, and should be repaired, cleaned and treated with a wood preservative every three to five years. You can also get them pretreated with a preservative or fire retardant, which gives them a life expectancy of 30 to 50 years. A zinc or copper strip applied at the roof ridge can also help wash wood shingles with a preservative when it rains. They are costlier than asphalt shingles or metal but comparable with tile.

- **Slate** This is an excellent roofing product, but not all slate stands up well in wet climates. It is low-maintenance, noncombustible and will last from 50 to 150 years. It is also the costliest choice.

Opposite: A deep roof overhang provides shade and protection from the elements on the terrace of a contemporary eco-friendly home by Eisner Design.

Above: The beautiful, budget-friendly horizontal cladding around the base of this newly constructed home is made from strips of reclaimed lodgepole pine.

Windows and Doors

Windows and doors play a vital role in defining the character of your home, but innovations in window and door technology have enabled these building components to play a more significant role in improving energy efficiency, too. While the ranges in styles and prices are vast, custom options give you even more control over their aesthetic and functional characteristics. For replacement windows in renovations or restorations, for example, some manufacturers, such as Marvin, provide options that allow you to precisely recreate a historic window while incorporating the latest energy-efficient glazing technology and frames, enabling you to install new windows with minimal disruption to interior surfaces and finishes. Others, such as Jeld-Wen, offer frame options made with sustainably harvested wood. Andersen, on the other hand, offers windows made from a new sustainable material

the company calls Fibrex, which is made from reclaimed wood fibers from their manufacturing process.

Most window and door manufacturers offer tools on their websites that can help you select new or replacement windows that suit your energy, aesthetic and budgetary requirements. From a green perspective, however, there are certain performance and toxicity issues that you should consider with your windows and doors.

• **Energy-efficiency and UV protection** To increase energy efficiency and comfort in your home, choose Energy Star–rated dual pane low-e windows. The panes of low-e windows have a metal-oxide coating that admits the sun's visible light but reflects infrared heat and ultraviolet rays in summer, cutting demand for cooling

Left: Architect Yianni Doulis used Ipe wood for this front porch deck and stairs and framed the pergola with FSC-certified cedar.
Above: High-performance oculus, clerestory and double-hung windows add character and function to a

home by Wesketch Architecture.
Opposite: Rot- and insect-resistant Western Red Cedar siding and a recycled steel solar shade make this home, built by McDonald Construction, beautiful and sustainable.

energy. In winter, indoor heat is reflected back into the house, reducing heating demand. The coating can be adapted to suit various climates. Also, the spaces between the panes of some windows are filled with argon, krypton or other nontoxic gases for more insulation. And in very cold climates, ask for windows with three or more panes. These qualities should also be sought in sidelights or decorative windows in exterior doors. If you're not in a position to purchase new windows, you can apply UV window film to your windows, which can help improve their effectiveness and efficiency. Various window film from 3M, for example, reduces the effects of solar heat and visible light on your furnishings; will block 99 percent of the sun's harmful ultraviolet rays and provide up to a 79 percent reduction in the sun's heat, reducing the cost of your energy bill.

- **Moisture issues** If the drainage channels of your windows aren't working properly, or if the windows are poorly installed with improper flashing, water can seep into the building cavity and cause structural damage. Have the windows tested for proper drainage during construction.

- **Materials and finishes** From a green perspective, there really is no perfect window frame. Vinyl and wood frames are more energy-efficient than aluminum frames, which

also require a lot of energy to produce. But vinyl frames off-gas and create toxicity issues during their manufacture and disposal. And since wood frames can be made from old-growth trees, they are often dipped in a fungicide, though they can be sealed to contain chemical exposure.

Chemically sensitive people should choose steel or aluminum windows with a baked-on finish. Most manufacturers also produce clad frames that have wood inside and steel, aluminum or fiberglass covering on the outside, which provides UV and weather protection and eliminates the need for maintenance with paints, seals and stains. That said, here are a few benefits of various types of frames:

- **Vinyl and fiberglass windows** work well and are relatively low priced and durable. If you decide on vinyl windows, choose good ones and make sure that they are installed to last so as to reduce manufacture of new ones and the amount of vinyl that ends up as waste. Fiberglass frames are also energy efficient and extremely durable.

- **Aluminum windows** have thinner frames than vinyl or wood windows and are available in a natural aluminum or a bronze/brown finish. They are a good choice for storm windows and new ones are assembled in a way that reduces "sweating," a drawback of the older versions.

that continuously outgas formaldehyde. To avoid chemical exposure from these types of doors, seal the door on all sides with a nontoxic sealer or primer, and paint with low-VOC products. And, if possible, choose doors made with solvent-free adhesives.

- **Weatherstripping** Doors with new frames may also include a magnetic strip to create a tighter seal that reduces air and water leakage and noise, and makes your home more energy efficient. Many types of weatherstripping are made from synthetic materials that outgas, such as neoprene, polypropylene nylon or urethane foam. Brass and stainless steel weatherstripping, available at many hardware stores, can be a less toxic alternative.

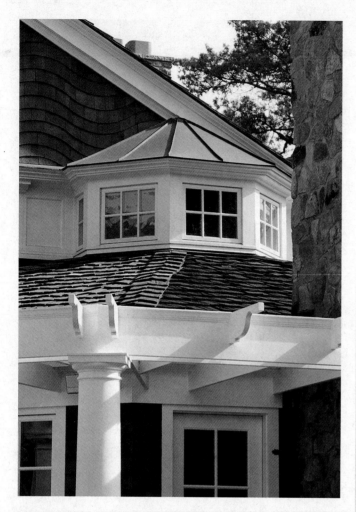

Energy-efficient dual-pane, low-e windows admit sunlight while screening out damaging infrared and ultraviolet rays.

- **Wood windows** are aesthetically appealing and their quality ranges from poor to outstanding. They also have the ability to replicate historic and traditional window styles. Good-quality wood windows are more expensive than vinyl and aluminum units.

DOORS

- **Frame and core** Wood cladding, fiberglass and steel doors with polyurethane foam cores are among the most energy-efficient exterior doors available. Solid and paneled wood doors are often made with toxic glues and treated with biocides. Fire-rated doors often contain particleboard cores

Window Replacement Dos and Don'ts

Replacing old windows may add value as well as energy efficiency to your house, but that is the hardest part to evaluate. An accurate calculation of the net value of windows in the sale of a home is almost impossible to ascertain and is one of the least compelling reasons to replace the windows in your home. Here, a few dos and don'ts on replacement:

- **Do** choose windows that are energy efficient, have operable sashes that open and shut easily, with frames that require very little maintenance or repair.

- **Don't** replace your windows just because there is a discount or some other weekly promotion.

- **Do** choose windows that can help reduce moisture and condensation problems and can be fitted with insect screens.

- **Don't** replace old leaded-glass or similar fine historic windows that can be maintained or repaired. If you are fortunate enough to have windows that add character to your home, have them restored and add storm windows to the outside.

- **Do** reuse the outer frame and trim of the existing windows if possible. To do this, remove the old glass and sashes. Carefully inspect the existing frames to make sure that they are in good condition and can last for the life of your new sashes. One area of frequent damage is the exterior windowsill. Small defects can be repaired. Insert the replacement window into the old sashes. Keeping the existing interior and exterior window trim can also save you money and help you preserve the style of your home.

SCREENS

In general, aluminum and stainless steel screens for windows and doors are preferable green options over fiberglass or nylon mesh screens, which can outgas and are often treated with pesticides.

Paints and Stains

Just as you would seek to finish interior walls or wood surfaces with low- or no-VOC paints and stains to enhance indoor air quality, exterior wood shingles, masonry and other siding should be treated with eco-friendly finishes, too. A new coat of exterior paint is functional—it protects the home from rain, snow, wind and sun damage. But in addition to improving the life of your home's skin, paint revives curb appeal and can pump up the value of a home.

As interest in green manufacturing processes and products increases, many eco-friendly exterior finish products are becoming available in the market, including Weather-Bos's nontoxic, low-VOC finishes made from natural oils and resins that penetrate deeply into wood, masonry and other materials. This provides protection not only from the elements, but from mold and mildew as well. Benjamin Moore's Aura exterior paint contains one of the lowest VOC (volatile organic compound) levels of any paint, exceeding the most stringent environmental regulations. It also provides unsurpassed performance, offers environmental safeguards, emits low odor and is specially formulated with agents that inhibit the growth of mildew.

Your architect should be able to help you sort through the eco-friendly options for the best product for your home's needs.

Peeling Paint Tip

A good exterior paint job should last 10 to 15 years. Premature paint deterioration is often the result of moisture and water vapor, which originates inside the home and penetrates through the wall and siding. If you see blistering or other paint deterioration on an exterior surface, one common cause is a failing tub or shower wall. This type of exterior paint damage cannot be corrected unless the cause of the moisture or water vapor is first eliminated and associated repairs are made. A careful inspection of the exterior and interior of the home should be performed before exterior siding and painting work begins.

Choosing Eco-Friendly Wood Building Products

- **Choose certified sustainably harvested wood.** To be sure that any wood you purchase has been sustainably harvested, demand that it be certified by a third-party organization accredited by the Forest Stewardship Council, the leading international organization that sets standards for green forestry and wood harvesting. To avoid problems with chemical sensitivity that treatments for mold, rot and pests can cause, choose wood from a certifier that uses the least toxic treatments. Also be sure the wood was kiln dried and is free of mold and mildew. If possible, choose fir, hemlock or spruce over pine or cedar, whose natural terpenes can be problematic for chemically sensitive people.

- **Choose benign wood treatments.** Woods are usually treated to prevent rot or insect or mold infestation. Some of the treatments, such as those that contain creosote and pentachlorophenol, are quite toxic. Instead, choose wood treated with BioShield, Bora-Care or low-toxicity treatments available on the market.

- **Choose healthy wood adhesives.** Wood adhesives can contain harmful solvents, so urge your architect and builder to work with healthier wood adhesives, such as Elmer's Carpenter Glue, Dap/Dow Corning silicone sealant and other safer glues.

- **Replace pressure-treated lumber.** During the last 25 years or so of the 20th century, lumber was pressure-treated with chromated copper arsenate or ammoniacal copper arsenate that is extremely toxic to humans and the environment. If you're remodeling and have decks or other structures made with this type of wood, try to safely remove it and replace it with a safer alternative. If you're building new, use a nontoxic alternative, such as Nature Wood, or other untreated or safely treated woods, especially for wood used as sill plates atop a stem or foundation wall.

- **Safely seal wood composite products,** such as truss joints, with a safe product such as B-I-N Primer Sealer to avoid VOC emissions into the home.

Living Healthily
and Energy-
Efficiently

HARVESTING AND SAVING ENERGY

It's practically impossible to imagine a world without electricity. We depend on it for so much of what we do. Since the first central power plant began generating electricity in our country in the 1880s, it has become our dominant energy form and powers the contemporary technologies that enhance our quality of life.

Today, American homes use more electricity than ever, which isn't surprising when you consider that the average U.S. household owns 25 consumer electronics products. In fact, the percentage of U.S. energy consumed in electric form has quadrupled since 1940. Electricity, for example, now powers more than 176 million personal computers and our national network of 208 million cellular phones, among a multitude of other appliances and home electronics. Furthermore, American homes are bigger than ever and use 21 percent more electricity today than they did in the late 1970s.

Despite enormous gains in energy efficiency, rapid population growth and an expanding digital economy will cause a substantial increase in electricity demand over the next 25 years. This means America's electric companies will need to generate more power to meet our demands for reliable electricity. At the same time, capacity margins are declining in most U.S. regions and, within the next 2 to 3 years, they will likely drop below minimum target levels in several areas of the country. The electricity delivery system—the transmission grid that delivers high-voltage electricity from generators to the distribution lines that reduce the voltage and deliver it to retail customers—is also overburdened. Furthermore, the delivery system has an aging infrastructure, largely reflecting technology developed more than 50 years ago.

The public debate over U.S. policy to address climate change is intensifying and Congress and policymakers continue to discuss what type of federal action or legislation is needed to reduce carbon dioxide and other greenhouse gas emissions. But no matter how we as a nation choose to address global warming, a sustained commitment by the electric power industry and policymakers to developing a wide range of technologies over several decades will be key in solving the problem.

While the electric power industry leads all other sectors in taking voluntary actions to reduce greenhouse gas emissions, about 49 percent of the fuel that America's electric companies rely on to generate electricity comes from coal, the burning of which contributes heavily to greenhouse gas emissions. But they also depend on a variety of other fuels, including nuclear energy, natural gas, fuel oil, and hydropower and other renewable sources. Fuel diversity protects everyone—electric companies and customers alike—from problems such as fuel unavailability, price fluctuations, and changes in regulatory practices that can drive up the cost of a particular fuel. Fuel diversity also helps ensure stability in the electricity supply.

From a green perspective, renewable energy sources—fuels that can be naturally replenished—are the fuels of choice to protect the planet. Hydropower is our nation's dominant renewable resource, providing 7 percent of total U.S. electricity supply. Non-hydro renewable energy sources—such as solar power, wind, geothermal power, and biomass—now generate only about 3 percent of the supply. But the electric power industry has expanded the use of non-hydro renewable energy resources for generating electricity during the last decade. Wind power is the fastest-growing renewable energy source, with wind farms currently operating in 32 states. A number of states also are encouraging the development of renewable energy resources based on their particular circumstances and available resources. To date, more than half the states in the U.S., plus the District of Columbia, have adopted mandatory renewable energy portfolio standards.

We can all play a role in fast-forwarding this transition. For example, the Alliance for Climate Protection, a nonprofit, nonpartisan effort founded by Nobel Laureate and former

vice president Al Gore, urges people to ask business and elected leaders to move toward a world powered by clean energy. Its leaders suggest starting by letting your utility company know that instead of coal power you want to buy solar, wind or geothermal energy; informing your mayor that you want city planning that encourages more efficient new buildings as well as sidewalks and bike paths; and asking state and national officials to develop policies that encourage investors to make long-term commitments to clean energy. According to the Alliance, a recent report has also shown that investment in a clean and efficient economy would "lead to over 3 million new green-collar jobs, stimulate $1.4 trillion in new GDP [gross domestic product], add billions in personal income and retail sales, produce $284 billion in net energy savings, all while generating sufficient returns to the U.S. Treasury to pay for itself over 10 years."

One effort called the Builders Challenge, which is spearheaded by the U.S. Department of Energy (DOE), is a step in the right direction. The program is a voluntary effort, challenging America's homebuilders to build 220,000 high-performance homes into the marketplace by 2012, and spurring strong consumer demand for these homes. The DOE's ultimate vision is to give consumers the opportunity to buy an affordable net zero energy home (NZEH)—a grid-connected home that, over the course of a year, produces as much energy as it uses—by 2030 anywhere in the United States.

Previous page: Natural light, efficient light fixtures and Energy Star–rated appliances contribute to an eco-friendly kitchen. Above: Energy-efficient windows can be custom made to mimic historical styles.

Simple Ways to Protect the Planet

You can save money and reduce your own contribution to global warming by making climate-friendly choices each day. Here are a few simple tips from the Alliance for Climate Protection for living a more climate-friendly life:

- Turn down or turn off the heat and air conditioning when you aren't home. Try using a programmable thermostat or setting your thermostat yourself to 68 degrees while you are awake and 60 degrees while you are asleep or away from home. In the summer, keep the thermostat at 78 degrees while you are at home, but give your air conditioning a rest when you are away. This will allow you to save about 10 percent a year on your home energy costs. If every house in America did this, our total greenhouse gas production would drop by about 35 million tons of CO_2. This is about the same as taking 6 million cars off the road.

- Choose energy-efficient appliances. Because they use less energy, Energy Star–rated appliances can reduce carbon pollution and have a big impact on your energy bill—just look for the Energy Star logo. Energy Star products typically exceed the federal energy standards by at least 15 percent. When buying appliances that use the most energy in your home, like heaters, air conditioners, water heaters and refrigerators, also use the Energy Guide card posted on the appliance to help you choose the one with the lowest annual energy consumption. Heating and cooling uses about half of the energy in a typical home and can account for about $1,500 in annual costs.

- Switch to compact fluorescent bulbs. According to the government's Energy Star program, if every American home replaced their five most-used light fixtures with Energy Star–rated compact fluorescents, the savings would add up to $8 billion annually in energy costs. That's like taking almost 10 million cars off the road. CFLs are widely available, affordable, and they last 10 times longer than traditional bulbs.

- Wash your clothes with cold water. If you usually use hot water for your laundry, you can cut your energy consumption in half by choosing warm water, and up to 90 percent if you choose cold. Your current liquid laundry detergent should work fine. If not, special cold-water detergents are available. Your clothes should be just as clean, and you'll thank yourself when the electricity bill arrives.

- Switch to green power. It is likely that most of the electricity you use comes from nonrenewable sources like coal. However, there are some utilities that will sell you climate-friendly electricity like wind, biomass or solar power if you ask for it. More than 750 utilities in 37 states offer green power products, and signing up can be very easy. To find out what your options are, check out the U.S. Department of Energy's map at: *eere.energy.gov/greenpower/buying/buying_power.shtml*, or contact your local energy company directly. And, when you sign up for green power, ask your utility when everyone will be getting clean energy.

For more information and ideas on how you can reverse the effects of climate change, visit the Alliance's website at *wecansolveit.org*.

Buying Clean Energy

According to the U.S. Department of Energy, the electricity industry is already undergoing a transformation. At least 50 percent of customers now have the option to purchase renewable electricity, also known as "green power" or "clean power," directly from their power supplier, and everyone has the option of purchasing renewable energy certificates. In most states, you can buy clean power through one or more of the following programs:

- **Green pricing** Some power companies now provide an optional green pricing service that allows customers to pay a small premium in exchange for electricity generated from clean, renewable energy sources.

- **Competitive electricity markets** Certain states have restructured their electricity industry to allow competition among electricity generators. In some of these states, clean power generators, who specialize in producing electricity using renewable sources, take advantage of the restructured market to sell clean power products to customers who will opt to pay slightly more for renewable energy products and services that reflect their environmental values.

- **Green certificates** More clean-power generators are now separating the power that they sell to power providers from the environmental attributes associated with that power. These environmental attributes are represented by "green

Halogen fixtures along with large windows and glass doors provide efficient natural and artificial illumination in this kitchen by Eisner Design.

certificates," "green tags," "renewable energy certificates" or "tradable renewable certificates." They are sold to companies and individuals who want to help increase the amount of clean power entering our nation's electricity supply. By separating the environmental attributes from the power, clean power generators can sell the electricity they produce to power providers at a competitive market value. Some of the extra revenue encourages the development of additional renewable energy projects. Many organizations offer green energy or renewable energy certificates that can be purchased separately from your current electricity service, too. The premium you pay for these options offsets the extra costs power companies incur in purchasing and/or generating electricity from renewable sources.

High-efficiency appliances complement bamboo-plywood cabinets and recycled pulls in the green kitchen of LEED-certified architect Rick Renner.

Types of Large-Scale Renewable Technologies

Renewable energy technologies can generate electricity on a large scale for residential, commercial and wholesale customers—and you may find that you can use one of the "green power" buying strategies to access them. These technologies include:

- **Hydropower** Currently the largest and least expensive source of renewable electricity produced in the United States, large- and small-scale hydropower projects are commonly used by clean-power generators to produce electricity, and account for 10 percent of the nation's electricity. Most hydropower projects use a dam and a reservoir to retain water from a river. Water stored in a reservoir can be accessed quickly for use during times when the demand for electricity is high. Used throughout the United States, hydropower is more common on the West Coast, especially in the northwestern United States.

- **Biomass** Biomass electrical generation, also known as biopower, is second only to hydropower as a renewable energy source. Most electricity generated using biomass is done through direct combustion using conventional boilers, which burn mostly waste wood products generated by the agriculture and wood-processing industries. Biomass resources are abundant across the eastern half of the United States, and thus, most operating biomass power plants are located there.

- **Concentrating solar power** Large-scale concentrating solar power technologies include parabolic troughs and power towers. Parabolic trough systems concentrate the sun's energy through long, rectangular curved reflectors that are tilted toward the sun, focusing the sun's energy on a pipe that runs down the center of the trough. The sun's energy heats oil flowing through the pipe, and the hot oil boils water in a conventional steam generator to produce electricity. They have a proven track record of functioning effectively for large-scale power needs and currently offer the least expensive way to produce solar electricity. Power towers have also shown their efficacy in demonstration projects, but they are not yet in use commercially. Concentrating solar power's relatively low cost and ability to deliver power during periods of peak demand means it can be a major contributor to the nation's future energy needs. These technologies function most efficiently in the southwestern United States, which receives the greatest amount of sun.

- **Geothermal** Heat from the Earth—geothermal energy—heats water that has seeped into underground reservoirs, and energy from high-temperature reservoirs (225°–600°F) can be used to produce electricity. There are currently three types of geothermal power plants:

  Dry steam plants use steam from underground wells to rotate a turbine, which activates a generator to produce electricity. Of the two known underground resources of steam in the United States, the Geysers in northern California and Old Faithful in Yellowstone National Park, the Geysers are the only source used for dry steam plants in the country, since Yellowstone is protected.

  Flash steam plants are the most common type of geothermal power plant and use waters at temperatures greater than 360°F. As the hot water flows up through wells, the decrease in pressure causes some of the water to boil into steam, which is used to power a generator.

  Binary cycle plants use the heat from lower-temperature reservoirs (225°–360°F) to boil a working fluid, which is then vaporized in a heat exchanger and used to power a generator. In the United States, geothermal energy has been used to generate electricity on a large scale since 1960 and is now becoming more cost-effective and competitive with fossil fuels. Current drilling technology limits the development of geothermal resources to relatively shallow water- or steam-filled reservoirs, most of which are found in the western part of the United States. But researchers are developing new technologies for capturing the heat in deeper, dry rocks, which would support drilling almost anywhere.

- **Photovoltaics (solar)** Solar cells, also called photovoltaics (PV), are used to economically power anything from watches and calculators to whole houses. PV technologies produce electricity directly from sunlight, which strikes a solar cell whose semiconductor materials absorb a portion of that light. Energy from the absorbed light then strikes electrons in the outer shell of an atom, freeing the electrons to travel into a circuit in the form of electricity.

The solar resource across the United States is ample for PV systems because they use both direct and scattered sunlight. But the amount of power generated by a PV system depends on how much of the sun's energy reaches it. As a result, PV systems—like other solar technologies—function best in the southwestern United States, which receives the most sunlight.

- **Wind** Many power providers use wind plants to supply power to their customers today. To meet the electricity needs of a power company, many large wind turbines are built close together to form a wind plant. Wind energy can be produced anywhere in the world where the wind blows with a strong and consistent force. Windier locations produce more energy, lowering the cost of producing electricity. Wind resources are found in most regions of the United States, but most usable wind resources in the U.S. are found in the western plains states.

Generating Your Own Clean Electricity

Some homeowners are actually beginning to generate electricity using their own small renewable energy systems. If you're willing to invest the time and money to research, buy and maintain it, a renewable energy system can be used to supply some or all of your electricity needs. If you use the electricity from your own system in place of electricity supplied by a power provider or electric utility, it is called a stand-alone or off-grid system. In remote locations, these systems can be more cost-effective than extending a power line to the electricity grid, which can cost from $15,000 to $50,000 per mile. You can also connect your system to the grid and use it to reduce the amount of conventional power supplied to you through the grid. Since the Public Utility Regulatory Policy Act requires power providers to purchase excess power from grid-connected, small renewable energy systems at a rate equal to what it costs the power provider to produce the power itself, a grid-connected system lets you sell whatever excess power you might produce back to your power provider.

Before you purchase and install a small renewable energy system, you'll need to understand and calculate your electricity loads to see if one of the small renewable energy systems can meet all or enough of your electricity needs. You'll also need to research your local codes and other requirements for installing such a system. In determining whether any of these technologies are viable for you, there are many variables to consider, including the size of your lot, zoning restrictions, wind speeds or sun conditions in your area, the cost and amount of electricity you use, whether your utility offers net metering, and the availability of state rebates and incentives. For more information on all of these technologies, visit the U.S. Department of Energy's Energy Efficiency and Renewable Energy website (*eere.energy.gov*).

If you plan to build a new home and a small renewable energy system is feasible for you, work with your architect, builder or contractor to incorporate the system into your whole house design. The renewable energy technologies available to generate your own electricity are similar to the large-scale technologies. These include small solar electric systems, small wind electric systems, micro-hydropower systems and small hybrid electric systems, which combine solar and wind technologies.

Opposite: Solar panels help supply energy to the urban home of architect Rick Renner, who added new insulation, triple-glazed windows, and efficient HVAC equipment.

Above: Innovative shingles from Eagle Roofing Products are actually solar collectors that harness energy while merging seamlessly with the design of the structure.

What Is a Net Zero Energy Home?

A Net Zero Energy Home combines state-of-the-art, energy-efficient construction and appliances with commercially available renewable energy systems, such as solar water heating and solar electricity. The combination results in a home that produces its own energy as much or more than it needs. Even though the home might be connected to a utility grid, it has net zero energy consumption from the utility provider. A Net Zero Energy Home can be designed to continue functioning even during blackouts, and the fact that such a home produces energy protects its owner from fluctuations in energy prices. It's also environmentally sustainable, as it saves energy and reduces pollution.

HEATING, VENTILATION AND AIR CONDITIONING

Heating and cooling systems account for more than half of the energy use in a typical U.S. home. To reduce the energy consumption and cost of cooling and heating, the first step is to maximize your home's efficiency. If you're remodeling your home, this means adding the recommended levels of insulation, installing energy-efficient windows and doors, applying weatherstripping, and sealing gaps and cracks in openings and joints with an eco-friendly caulk. If you're building a new green home, it means siting and designing your home in a way that maximizes passive heating and cooling techniques, and creating an envelope that is tight and efficient.

Once you've done this, decide on the type of system you want and work with a contractor to figure out the optimum size for it. If you're thinking of replacing or upgrading an existing heating and cooling system, first learn about the limitations of your current system and available energy sources in your area. When choosing a system for a new house, you'll have a wider array of options.

Selecting a System

There are a lot of technologies available for heating and cooling your home, each with advantages and disadvantages. In addition, many heating and cooling systems have supporting equipment, such as thermostats and electric or gas meters, which provide additional opportunities for saving energy. When choosing a heating and cooling system, there is no perfect answer. Choosing between systems depends in part on your fuel options, but also on your preferences.

Cooling Systems

Depending on where you live, cooling your home can be as simple as opening a window or as complicated as installing a central air-conditioning unit. Here is a summary of the most common options:

Ventilation Except in hot, humid climates, natural ventilation is the cheapest and most energy-efficient way to cool a home. In some cases, natural ventilation will suffice for cooling, although it usually needs to be supplemented with spot ventilation, ceiling fans and window fans. For large homes, consider whole-house fans. In hot climates, attic ventilation can help to reduce the use of air conditioning.

Evaporative Coolers In low-humidity areas, evaporating water into the air provides a natural, energy-efficient means of cooling. Evaporative coolers, also known as swamp coolers, rely on this principal. Evaporative coolers cost about half as much to install as central air conditioners and use about a quarter as much energy. They are higher-maintenance than refrigerated air conditioners, though, and are suitable only for low-humidity areas.

Air conditioners Two-thirds of all homes in the U.S. are equipped with air conditioners. They use about 5 percent of all the electricity produced in the country, costing homeowners more than $11 billion and releasing roughly 100 million tons of carbon dioxide into the air each year. Switching to high efficiency air conditioners and using other means to cool your home can reduce this energy use by 20 to 50 percent. The two most common types of air conditioners are room air conditioners and central air conditioners. Ductless, mini-split air conditioners provide a compromise between these two systems.

Low-Impact Cooling Tricks

When it's hot outside, our first instinct is to turn on the air conditioner. But they guzzle energy. Using non-AC cooling strategies saves both money and the planet. Here, a few tips for keeping cool without touching the thermostat.

- Open windows and interior doors to allow air to flow freely through your house. Closed interior doors reduce air flow.
- Replace incandescent lightbulbs with compact fluorescents (CFLs), which give off 75 percent less heat.
- Install a whole-house fan and turn it on at the end of the day, when it begins to cool off outside.
- Plant deciduous trees on the south, east and west sides of your home to block the sun and keep the house cooler.
- Install window shades or curtains and keep them closed during the day to prevent direct sunlight from entering the house.
- If you're renovating or building, try creating an open floor plan to encourage airflow.

Opposite: A sleek, straightforward ceiling fan over the kitchen area provides low-tech ventilation in this open-plan space.

Above: The R-value of the windows almost equals that of this home's soy-based-foam-insulated walls, minimizing the need for cooling.

Heating Systems

Most U.S. homes use either a furnace or a boiler, but other approaches range from woodstoves to active solar heating systems. Whether you want to upgrade an existing system or purchase a new one, there are various fuel- and energy-related issues that will influence your decision. Here is a summary of most of the options.

FURNACES AND BOILERS

Furnaces heat air, which is then distributed through the house via ducts. Boilers heat water, providing either hot water or steam for heating. High-efficiency versions of all types of furnaces and boilers are available, and since they are safer and can be more than 30 percent more efficient than the older systems, upgrading to a new system can cut your fuel bills and your furnace's pollution output in half. Despite their high efficiency, however, the higher cost of electricity in most parts of the country makes all-electric furnaces or boilers a poor choice financially.

Since retrofits are fuel-specific, any new system you purchase will need to be geared to the fuel you use. Other retrofitting options that can improve a system's energy efficiency include installing programmable thermostats, upgrading ductwork for forced-air systems and adding zone control for hot-water systems. Before buying a new furnace or boiler or modifying your existing unit, have a heating contractor size your furnace so that you make the correct choice, and choose a high-efficiency furnace and boiler with the Energy Star label. If you live in a cold climate, it usually makes sense to invest in the highest-efficiency system. In milder climates with lower annual heating costs, the extra investment can be harder to justify.

To ensure that any new furnace or boiler remains effective, you should have it inspected and maintained by a heating system professional. And anytime you maintain, retrofit or replace a gas heating system, check for unintentional air leaks, or problems with air ducts that connect to the outdoors. The combustion process creates byproducts that can be hazardous to human health and impact the air quality in your home. Ensure that your chimney system functions properly and that a gas heating system is properly ventilated. Installing a sealed-combustion furnace or boiler can also help. If you replace an older furnace or boiler with a higher-efficiency new system,

the chimneys must be prepared to accommodate it. Also, contact your local utility or heating contractor to check for and remedy any other venting problems, such as the presence of high-temperature plastic vent pipe, which has been recalled and should be replaced by stainless steel vent pipe.

WOOD AND PELLET HEATING

Before the 20th century, most Americans burned wood to heat their homes. But the use of fossil fuels increased over time, and by 1970, only 1 percent of the population used wood for fuel. During the energy crisis in the 1970s, however, interest in wood heating as a renewable energy grew. Later, pellet fuel appliances, which burn small pellets made from compacted sawdust, wood chips, bark, agricultural crop waste, waste paper and other organic materials, emerged. Today you can find a new generation of wood- and pellet-burning appliances that are cleaner-burning, more efficient and powerful enough to heat many average-sized modern homes.

Since wood-burning appliances and fireplaces may emit large quantities of air pollutants, some municipalities restrict their use when the local air quality reaches unacceptable levels. Others restrict or ban the installation of wood-burning appliances in new construction. Before installing a wood-burning system, contact your local building codes department, state energy office or state environmental agency about wood-burning regulations that may apply in your area.

If you have an older wood-burning appliance, consider upgrading to one of the new varieties certified by the U.S. Environmental Protection Agency (EPA). These include a catalytic combustor that allows combustion gases to burn at lower temperatures, thereby cleaning the exhaust gas while generating more heat. High-efficiency appliances are also often safer, since complete combustion helps to prevent a buildup of flammable chimney deposits called creosote. New catalytic stoves and inserts have advertised efficiencies of 70 to 80 percent.

If you want to retrofit an existing non-catalytic wood-burning appliance with a catalytic combustor, you can buy a catalytic damper—though they don't work for all types of stoves. For safety, and to maximize efficiency, have a professional install your wood- or pellet-burning appliance.

Types of Wood- and Pellet-Burning Appliances

• **High-efficiency fireplaces and fireplace inserts** Designed more for show, traditional open-masonry fireplaces should not be considered heating devices. Only high-efficiency fireplace inserts have proven effective in increasing the heating efficiency of older fireplaces. But some modern fireplaces heat at efficiencies near those of woodstoves and are certified as low-emission appliances. Although designed to include the fire-viewing benefits of a traditional fireplace, this generation of fireplaces can effectively provide heat as well. Fireplace flues leak heat and warm air out of your

home, however. If you have a fireplace that you don't use, plug and seal the flue. If you use the fireplace, be sure to close the flue when the fireplace is not in use.

• **Catalytic Woodstoves, Advanced Combustion Woodstoves, and Centralized Wood-Burning Boilers** Woodstoves are the most common appliances for burning wood. Advanced combustion woodstoves provide a lot

Opposite: Solar photovoltaic panels supply most of the energy for the radiant hydronic heating system that warms this house. A natural-gas system, which fuels the built-in fireplace, serves as a backup if necessary.

Left: An EcoSmart Fire open fireplace is flue-less, requires no utility connection, and uses clean-burning, renewable denatured ethanol. Above: Skylights allow sunlight to warm this fireplace's stone facing and radiate heat back into the room.

of heat but only work efficiently when the fire burns at full throttle. Also known as secondary burn stoves, they can reach temperatures of 1100°F—hot enough to burn combustible gases. New advanced combustion stoves have advertised efficiencies of 60 to 72 percent. They can also be slightly less expensive than conventional woodstoves fitted with catalytic combustors. Like woodstoves, centralized wood-burning boilers have been improved recently. Modern, centralized wood heaters use wood gasification technology that burns both the wood fuel and the associated combustible gases, and these are up to 80 percent efficient.

- **Masonry heaters** Masonry heaters—also known as Russian, Siberian, or Finnish fireplaces—produce more heat and less pollution than any other wood- or pellet-burning appliance. Masonry heaters include a firebox, a large masonry mass (such as bricks), and long, twisting smoke channels that run through the masonry mass. Masonry heaters commonly reach a combustion efficiency of 90 percent. Most are intended for burning wood. Their relatively small, intense fire also results in very little air pollution and very little creosote buildup in the chimney. In addition, if the masonry heater is built where sunlight can directly shine on it in winter, the heater will absorb the sun's heat and release it slowly into the room. They can be custom-built or purchased as prefabricated units. Some large designs may cost $5,000 or more. Plans and kits are available, but they are not easy do-it-yourself projects.

- **Pellet-Fuel Appliances** These are more convenient to operate and have much higher combustion and heating efficiencies than ordinary woodstoves or fireplaces. As a result, they produce very little air pollution and are the cleanest of solid fuel–burning residential heating appliances. With combustion efficiencies of 78 to 85 percent, they are also exempt from EPA smoke-emission testing requirements. Pellet stoves have heating capacities that range between 8,000 and 90,000 Btu per hour and can be used in homes as well as apartments or condominiums. Most pellet stoves cost between $1,700 and $3,000. However, a pellet stove is often cheaper to install than a cordwood-burning heater. Many can be direct-vented and do not need an expensive chimney or flue.

CHIMNEYS AND MAINTENANCE

If you are designing or building a new home, consider placing the chimney inside your home. Traditional chimneys constructed along the outside of a home lose valuable heat to the cold outside air. Chimneys must also match the size of the appliance. High-performance chimneys are insulated. Older masonry chimneys can be relined to safely and efficiently connect to newer high-efficiency wood-burning appliances.

To keep your wood- or pellet-burning system operating efficiently and safely, you'll need to maintain it on a regular basis. Every year before heating season, have a chimney sweep certified by the Chimney Safety Institute of America inspect your wood-burning system.

ELECTRIC RESISTANCE HEATING

Electric resistance heating converts almost 100 percent of the energy in the electricity that powers it to heat. But most electricity is produced from oil, gas or coal generators that convert only about 30 percent of the fuel's energy into electricity. Because of these losses, electric heat is often more expensive than heat produced using combustion appliances, such as natural gas, propane and oil furnaces. If electricity is the only choice, opt if you can for a heat pump, which is preferable in many climates. It can easily cut electricity use by 50 percent compared to electric resistance heating.

Types of Electric Resistance Heaters

Electric resistance heat can be supplied by centralized forced-air electric furnaces or by heaters in each room. These may be electric baseboard heaters, electric wall heaters, electric radiant heat, electric space heaters or electric thermal storage systems.

- **Electric Baseboard Heaters** These are zone heaters containing electric heating elements encased in metal pipes that are controlled by thermostats within each room. The quality of baseboard heaters varies considerably. To be sure your unit complies with recognized safety standards, look for labels from Underwriters Laboratories (UL) and the National Electrical Manufacturer's Association (NEMA).

- **Electric Wall Heaters** Electric wall heaters typically consist of an electric element with a reflector that projects heat into the room and a fan that moves air through the heater.

They are usually installed on interior walls because they're difficult to insulate on exterior walls.

- **Electric Furnaces** Electric furnaces are more expensive to operate than other electric resistance systems because of heat losses through their ducts and the extra energy needed to distribute the heated air throughout your home.

- **Electric Thermal Storage** Some electric utilities structure their rates like telephone companies and charge more for electricity during the day and less at night in an attempt to reduce their peak demand. If you are a customer of such a utility, you may be able to benefit from an electric thermal storage heater, which stores electric heat during nighttime hours when rates are lower. It doesn't save energy, but it can save you money. There are several types of electric thermal storage heaters, so you'd need to explore the kind that would work best for you.

All types of electric resistance heating are controlled through some kind of thermostat, which can be programmable and allow you to automatically set back the temperature at night or while you're away. Zone heating can produce energy savings of more than 20 percent compared to heating both occupied and unoccupied areas of your house.

A geothermal system buried in the yard provides the heating and cooling needs for this home designed by Wesketch Architecture.

ACTIVE SOLAR HEATING

There are two basic types of active solar heating systems: liquid-based systems, which heat water or an antifreeze solution in a hydronic collector, and air-based systems, which heat air in an air collector. Both systems collect and absorb solar radiation, then transfer the solar heat directly to an interior space or to a storage system from which the heat is distributed. If the system cannot provide adequate space heating, an auxiliary or backup system provides the additional heat. Liquid systems are more often used when storage is included, and are well-suited for radiant heating systems, boilers with hot water radiators, and absorption heat pumps and coolers. Both air and liquid systems can also supplement forced-air systems.

Active solar heating systems are most cost-effective when they are used for most of the year—that is, in cold climates with good solar resources—and when they're are used to displace more expensive heating fuels, such as electricity, propane and oil heat. Some states offer sales tax exemptions, income tax credits or deductions, and property tax exemptions or deductions for solar energy systems. Heating your home with an active solar energy system can also significantly reduce your fuel bills in the winter, and the amount of air pollution and greenhouse gases that result from your use of fossil fuels such as oil, propane and natural gas for heating.

A radiant heating system beneath the stone floor warms this indoor/outdoor space, allowing the area to be enjoyed during the cooler months.

Selecting the appropriate solar energy system depends on the site, design and heating needs of your house. Local covenants may also restrict your options. The local climate, the type and efficiency of the collector, and the collector area determine how much heat a solar heating system can provide. Designing an active system to supply enough heat 100 percent of the time is usually neither practical nor cost-effective, so most building codes and mortgage lenders require a backup heating system to supply heat when the solar system cannot meet requirements.

Once a system is in place, it has to be properly maintained to optimize its performance and avoid breakdowns. Different systems require different types of maintenance, but you should figure on 8 to 16 hours of maintenance annually.

RADIANT HEATING

Radiant heating systems supply heat directly to the floor or to panels in the wall or ceiling of a house. They are more efficient than baseboard heating and usually more efficient than forced air heating because no energy is lost through ducts. The lack of moving air can also be advantageous to people with severe allergies. Radiant floor heating systems are different than the radiant panels used in walls and ceilings.

Radiant Floor Heat

There are three types of radiant floor heat: radiant air floors, electric radiant floors, and hot water or hydronic radiant floors. All three types can be further subdivided by the type of installation: those that make use of the large thermal mass of a concrete slab floor or lightweight concrete over a wooden subfloor—these are called wet installations—and those in which the installer sandwiches the radiant floor tubing between two layers of plywood or attaches the tubing under the finished floor or subfloor—these are dry installations.

TYPES OF RADIANT FLOOR HEAT

- **Air-Heated Radiant Floors** Because air cannot hold large amounts of heat, radiant air floors are not cost-effective in residential applications, and are seldom installed.
- **Hydronic Radiant Floors** Hydronic systems are the most popular and cost-effective radiant heating systems for climates that require high levels of heat. These systems pump heated water from a boiler through tubing laid in

a pattern underneath the floor. The cost of installing a hydronic radiant floor varies by location and also depends on the size of the home, the type of installation and the floor covering. Hydronic systems use little electricity, a benefit for homes off the power grid or in areas with high electricity prices. These systems can also be heated with a wide variety of energy sources, including standard gas- or oil-fired boilers, wood-fired boilers, solar water heaters or some combination of these heat sources.

- **Electric Radiant Floors** Electric radiant floors typically consist of electric cables built into the floor or mats of electrically conductive plastic mounted onto the subfloor below a floor covering such as tile. Because of the relatively high cost of electricity, electric radiant floors are usually only cost-effective if they include a significant thermal mass, such as a thick concrete floor, and if your electric utility company offers time-of-use rates, allowing you to charge the concrete floor with heat during off-peak hours.

FLOOR INSTALLATION AND COVERING OPTIONS

Ceramic tile is the most common and effective floor covering for radiant floor heating because it conducts heat well and adds thermal storage due to its high heat capacity. Other floor coverings like vinyl and linoleum sheet goods, carpeting or wood can also be used, but any covering that helps to insulate the floor from the room will decrease the efficiency of the system. If you want to use carpeting, opt for a thin carpet with dense padding and install as little carpeting as possible. If you use wood flooring, choose laminated flooring instead of solid wood to reduce the possibility of the wood shrinking and cracking.

Radiant Panel Heat

Wall- and ceiling-mounted radiant panels are usually made of aluminum and can be heated with either electricity or with tubing that carries hot water, which can create issues with leakage. Most radiant panels for homes are electrically heated. Like any type of electric heat, radiant panels are expensive to operate, but they can provide supplemental heating in some rooms or can provide heat to a home addition when extending the conventional heating system is impractical.

Unlike other types of radiant heating systems, radiant panels have very low heat capacity, but they have the quickest response time of any heating technology. Because the panels can be individually controlled for each room, the quick-response feature can potentially result in cost and energy savings compared to other systems when rooms are infrequently occupied. But as with any system, the thermostat must be maintained at a minimum temperature that will prevent pipes from freezing.

HEAT PUMP SYSTEMS

For climates with moderate heating and cooling needs, heat pumps offer an energy-efficient alternative to furnaces and air conditioners and offer the benefit of delivering more useful energy than they consume.

Heat pumps use electricity to move heat from cool to warm spaces, making the cool space cooler and the warm space warmer. During the heating season, heat pumps move heat from the cool outdoors into your warm house; during the cooling season, they do the reverse. Because they move heat rather than generate it, heat pumps can provide up to four times the amount of energy they consume.

Types of Heat Pumps

• **Air-source heat pumps** The most common type of heat pump is the air-source heat pump, which transfers heat between your house and the outside air. If you heat with electricity, a heat pump can trim the amount of electricity you use for heating by as much as 30 to 40 percent. High-efficiency heat pumps also dehumidify better than standard central air conditioners, cutting energy usage and providing more cooling comfort in summer months. Most air-source heat pumps are unsuitable for cold climates, however, but there are systems that work in such environments.

For homes without ducts, air-source heat pumps come in a ductless version called a mini-split heat pump. In addition, a special type of air-source heat pump called a reverse cycle chiller generates hot and cold water rather than air, allowing it to be used with radiant systems in heating mode.

Left, top to bottom: Vanguard Energy Partners retrofitted the historic Twin Maples show house with a geothermal heat pump system.

Opposite: Windows covered with simple Roman shades supplement the illumination and heating of this home with a passive solar approach.

- **Geothermal heat pumps** Geothermal (ground-source or water-source) heat pumps, which transfer heat between your house and the ground or a nearby water source, achieve higher efficiencies but they cost more to install. They have low operating costs, though, because they take advantage of relatively constant ground or water temperatures.

- **Absorption heat pumps** An absorption heat pump, also called a gas-fired heat pump, is a new type of heat pump for residential systems. It uses heat as its energy source, and can be driven with a wide variety of heat sources.

CHOOSING A HEATING FUEL

Selecting the fuel and heating system best suited for your needs depends on the availability and cost of the fuel and the type of appliance you're using or want to use. It also depends on how heat is distributed in your house and your concern with the environmental impacts associated with the heating fuel.

Fuel Availability

Most homeowners see themselves as relatively limited in their options for heating fuels. In the Northeast, the options are essentially fuel oil or electricity, although natural gas is becoming

available to more homes. In rural areas, heating fuels are mostly limited to propane and wood. In most of the rest of the country, natural gas and electricity are the main choices. But the options are actually more diverse. For starters, solar energy is available throughout the country, and new homes in cold or moderate climates can always be designed to exploit passive solar heating strategies. You can also use active solar heating systems as a supplemental heating source in new or existing homes, as they're compatible with most heating systems. Pellet and propane fuels are also available nationwide at competitive prices, as is wood, which is especially cost-effective if you can harvest it yourself.

Fuel Costs

A simple way to evaluate heating options is to compare the cost of the fuel. To do that, you have to know the energy content of the fuel and the efficiency by which it can be converted to useful heat. The efficiency of the heating appliance is another important factor when determining the cost of a given amount of heat. In general, the efficiency is determined by measuring how well an appliance turns fuel into useful heat.

You can use several evaluation tools at the U.S. Department of Energy's website *(see sidebar page 88)* to help

HVAC Upgrade and Retrofit Tips

- Consider switching from electric to hot-water heating. The expense for ducting can make upgrading to a ducted system prohibitively expensive, but if you switch to a hot water baseboard system, you may be able to install it in the same location as your existing baseboards. It will require extensive plumbing, however.

- Upgrade steam heating by upgrading or replacing your boiler. In newer two-pipe steam systems it is sometimes possible to convert existing steam distribution pipes to hot water heating, which reduces the cost of the system to the cost of the boiler, the baseboard heaters and the installation labor. The space-saving benefits of eliminating the large steam radiators may be worth the expense.

- Add central AC to a ducted system. If you don't already have it, adding central air conditioning to a forced-air heating system is fairly simple, but your contractor must match the system to your existing ductwork.

- Add AC to a ductless system. Many homes that use steam or hot water heating, radiant heating, or electric resistance heating do not have ducts. If you want to add central air conditioning, consider instead adding a ductless mini-split air conditioner or ductless mini-split heat pump.

- Switch to a heat pump system. Switching to a heat pump system can be problematic, since heat pumps generally require larger ducts. However, many heating systems are oversized, particularly if your home is well insulated. You may be able to convert to a smaller-capacity heat pump that complements your existing ductwork. A heating and cooling professional can help you confirm whether or not this is possible.

- Install a mini-duct air distribution system. Adding ducts to an existing home can be a difficult proposition. But new mini-duct systems, which force air through plastic feeder ducts that are only 2 inches in diameter, can be easily threaded through cavities in walls, floors and ceilings. A heating and cooling professional should be able to help you evaluate the options.

you calculate the cost of energy delivered to your home for different fuels and systems, and find out the average efficiencies for common heating appliances. Or you can contact your utility or local suppliers of other fuels to get comparisons.

Environmental Impact of Fuels

Since you probably generate more greenhouse gases by heating and cooling your home than by doing anything else, you'll also want to consider the environmental impact of your heating fuel. Most electricity in the U.S. is generated by burning coal, which emits sulfur dioxide, nitrous oxides, particulates and greenhouse gases. While some electricity is generated from natural gas, which burns cleaner, at least half of the energy is lost in converting it to electricity and delivering it to your home. However, electric heat pumps, which have the benefit of producing more energy than they consume, can balance out the efficiency losses by using the electricity to draw energy from the environment.

Among the fuel options for a high-efficiency furnace or boiler—natural gas, oil, propane, wood or pellets—natural gas burns cleanest. But the cleanest fuel for heating (and possibly cooling) your home is solar energy, which produces no pollution at all. While solar energy just supplements the main heating and cooling source in most homes today, the Department of Energy and other developers are experimenting with building homes that aim to consume net zero energy over the course of a year.

Designed by Plumbob and built by McDonald Constrcution, this home incorporates thoughtful passive solar design strategies, with lots of glass to let in plenty of warming sunlight in winter as the sun sinks in the sky, and deep overhangs and sunshades to block heat and excess light in summer. Interior shades on the windows also control light and heat gain.

WATER CONSERVATION, FILTRATION AND HEATING

With rising energy prices and concern about greenhouse gases, those of us concerned with the environment tend to focus on reduction of the use of fossil fuels as a source for energy. But Americans across the country are also stretching our available water supplies to the limits. Since 1950, the U.S. population has nearly doubled, but since that time, public demand for water has more than tripled, and Americans now use an average of 100 gallons of water each day. This increased demand has stressed our water supplies and distribution systems, threatening both human health and the environment, making water conservation a national priority. According to the EPA, a recent government survey showed at least 36 states are anticipating local, regional or statewide water shortages by 2013.

The water used for residential, commercial, industrial and public uses, such as street cleaning, fire fighting, municipal parks and public swimming pools, comes from both publicly supplied sources and self-supplied sources (water withdrawn directly from surface or ground water, such as from privately owned wells). Only 15 percent of American households are self-supplied, while more than 240 million people depend on public supply systems.

More than 43 billion gallons are withdrawn for public supply systems every day, with nearly 60 percent of the public supply being delivered to households (self-supplied water to households totals about 4 billion gallons per day). Most people in North America use 50 to 70 gallons of water indoors each day and about the same amount outdoors, depending on the season. Indoors, about 75 percent of the water is used in the bathroom, and the toilet accounts for about 28 percent of that water use. Outdoors, water for lawns and gardens as well as for car washing accounts for most of the water used. Running a sprinkler for two hours, for example, can use up to 500 gallons, while washing a driveway with a hose uses up about 50 gallons of water every 5 minutes.

Above: A sleek faucet and showerhead complement the simplicity of this bath by Michelle Kaufmann Designs and conserve water, too.

Opposite: Cabinets in this bath are made of Kirei Board, a sustainable material made from sorghum plants. A wall-mounted, water-conserving faucet keeps the counter surface clear.

Water Conservation

Fortunately, manufacturers of household fixtures, fittings and appliances that use, condition or process water are creating more sophisticated, energy-efficient, conservation-oriented products than ever before. And the EPA's WaterSense program is making it easier to identify water-efficient products and practices so that we can help preserve water supplies for future generations, while saving money and protecting the environment at the same time.

Putting forth the effort to use water more efficiently along with reducing pollutants, such as pesticides, can benefit the planet in many ways. The EPA lists the following as just a few:

- Fewer sewage system failures caused from excess water use overwhelming the system.

- Reduced water contamination from polluted runoff due to over-irrigating agricultural and urban lands.

- Reduced need to construct additional dams and reservoirs or otherwise regulate the natural flow of streams, thus preserving their free flow and retaining the value of stream and river systems as wildlife habitats and recreational areas.

- Reduced need to construct additional water and wastewater treatment facilities.

- Reduced amount of energy needed to treat wastewater, resulting in less energy demand and, therefore, fewer harmful byproducts from power plants.

Most of us recognize that hot water demands a substantial use of energy, but supplying and treating cold water requires plenty of energy too. According to the EPA, American public

than 60 billion gallons of water each year. Doing so would also help us save money on water bills. To get a sense of the energy consumed by water usage, running your faucet for five minutes uses about as much energy as letting a 60-watt lightbulb run for 14 hours.

To get the most efficient product for your needs, you'll need to do some homework. For more information on water-conserving products, from sink faucets and showerheads to toilets and irrigation control technologies, visit the Water Sense section of the EPA's website (*epa.gov/watersense*).

Water Filtration

In addition to conservation, controlling the safety and quality of our drinking water is also important. Most of us assume the tap water in our homes is safe to drink. And, in general, municipal water supplies in our country are of good quality. But a few years, ago, the Natural Resources Defense Council (NRDC) issued a report on tap water quality in 19 U.S. cities and five of them rated poor.

To get a sense of the water quality in your area, read your municipal water report. The Safe Drinking Water Act requires municipal agencies to issue a water quality report listing levels of detected contaminants in the water supply, which is sent to households once a year with the water bill. If you're among the 15 percent of the U.S. population that relies on private water sources, these are not subject to the EPA's safe drinking water standards. For these sources, the EPA recommends having well water tested annually for coliform bacteria, nitrates and other possible contaminants.

water supply and treatment facilities consume about 56 billion kilowatt-hours per year—enough electricity to power more than 5 million homes for a year. The EPA also suggests that if just 1 percent of American homes replaced an old toilet with a Water Sense-labeled toilet, the country would save more than 38 million kilowatt-hours of electricity—enough electricity to supply 43,000 households for a month. By the same token, if every household in America installed a Water Sense-labeled faucet or aerator, we could save more

Above, and opposite, left: Using a Water-Sense labeled adapter aerates the water coming from any showerhead, saving about a gallon a minute. Opposite top and bottom:

Caroma's Caravelle dual-flush toilet uses less than a gallon of water per flush. American Standard's FloWise showerhead has three spray settings and reduces water consumption by 40 percent.

Above: Moen's ChoiceFlo faucet offers two waterways. Unfiltered water for boiling or cleaning up flows through the primary spout, while filtered water for washing greens or drinking passes through a special outlet beneath the neck.

Simple Steps to Save Water

Aside from replacing water-guzzling appliances, fixtures and fittings with efficient models, try these other simple steps for conserving water from the EPA's WaterSense program and Eartheasy.com, a website with information, tips and product ideas that support sustainable living:

- **Fix any leaks.** Leaky faucets dripping at a rate of one drip per second can waste more than 3,000 gallons of water each year. If you're unsure whether you have a leak, read your water meter before and after a two-hour period when no water is being used. If the meter doesn't read exactly the same, you probably have a leak. A leaky toilet can waste about 200 gallons of water every day. To determine whether your toilet has a leak, place a drop of food coloring in the tank; if the color shows in the bowl without flushing, you have a leak.

- **Take a shower, not a bath.** A full bathtub requires about 70 gallons of water, while a five-minute shower uses just 10 to 25 gallons. If you take a bath, stopper the drain first and adjust the water temperature as you fill the tub.

- **Control your faucet.** The average bathroom faucet flows at a rate of two gallons per minute. If you turn off the tap while brushing your teeth or shaving, you can save up to 8 gallons of water per day, or 240 gallons a month.

- **Water wisely.** A typical single-family suburban household uses 40 percent of its water outdoors for irrigation. Some experts estimate that more than 50 percent of landscape water use goes to waste due to evaporation or runoff from overwatering. Drip irrigation systems use between 20 to 50 percent less water than conventional in-ground sprinkler systems.

- **Load it up.** The average washing machine uses about 41 gallons of water per load. High-efficiency washing machines use less than 28 gallons of water per load. To achieve even greater savings, wash only full loads of laundry or use the appropriate load size selection on the washing machine.

- **Don't flush money down the drain.** If your toilet was made in 1992 or earlier, you probably have an inefficient model that uses at least 3.5 gallons per flush. New and improved high-efficiency models use less than 1.3 gallons per flush—at least 60 percent less than their older counterparts. Compared to a toilet that uses 3.5 gallons per flush, a WaterSense-labeled toilet could save a family of four more than $90 annually on their water bill, and $2,000 over the lifetime of the toilet.

- **Put a float booster in your toilet tank.** To cut down on water waste, buy an inexpensive tank bank or float booster, which may save 10 or more gallons of water per day.

- **Insulate your water pipes.** It's easy and inexpensive to insulate your water pipes with pre-slit foam pipe insulation. You'll get hot water faster plus avoid wasting water while it heats up.

- **Install water-saving showerheads and low-flow faucet aerators.** Inexpensive water-saving showerheads or restrictors are easy to install. For less than $15, you can install one of these yourself and save up to 500 gallons per year. Also, limit your showers to the time it takes to soap up, wash down and rinse off.

- **Wash sensibly.** Aside from fully loading dishwashers and clothes washers for optimum water conservation, avoid pre-rinsing dishes to save water, and if possible do not wash dishes by hand. The water in a sink doesn't get hot enough to kill bacteria, and leaving water running for rinsing wastes water. Also, avoid the permanent press cycle on the clothes washer, which uses an extra 5 gallons for the additional rinse.

Home Water Treatment Devices

There are several water filtration/treatment products that can be used in the home. Here is a summary:

- **Activated Carbon Filter** Improves taste and color, but does not remove bacteria, nitrates or dissolved minerals. Available in various point-of-use designs, some of which remove lead, copper, mercury, chlorination byproducts and pesticides.

- **Distillation** Removes bacteria, nitrates, sodium, hardness, heavy metals and radionuclides, but does not remove some VOCs. Available in whole-house or point-of-use designs.

- **Ion Exchange** Removes minerals, softens water, and some designs remove radium, barium, fluoride and/or arsenate. Available in whole-house or point-of-use designs.

- **Reverse Osmosis** Improves taste and color, and removes nitrates, sodium and other dissolved minerals, plus certain parasites. Some versions reduce dioxins, pesticides, chloroform and petrochemicals. Under-sink system.

- **Ultraviolet disinfection** Kills bacteria and parasites. Under-sink system.

Even if your water is clean, it can pick up contaminants from pipes leading to or in the home. From a green perspective, none of the pipe options available today are perfect. Some pre-WWII houses may still have original lead-based supply pipes, and copper supply pipes installed before 1988 might have lead-based solder that leaches into the water supply. Since lead can cause serious harm to the brain, nervous system and kidneys, have your water tested if you suspect that your pipes may be a problem. Copper pipes are safer, but mining for copper disrupts the environment, and at certain pH levels, copper can also leach into the water supply. Various plastic piping used for potable water, including PVC (polyvinyl chloride) and HDPE (high-density polyethylene) among others, outgas and can cause potentially harmful effects to humans. All plastic piping for potable water must now be certified by the National Sanitation Foundation (NSF) for health and environmental quality. Polypropylene piping is considered one of the cleanest plastic pipes and was recently approved by the International Plumbing Code and the International Residential Code. Your county government or local health department can give a list of state-certified testing labs to analyze the quality of your pipes.

If you can't replace your pipes, you can install a home water-treatment system that will improve the quality of the water, though no system eliminates all contaminants. Whole-house systems or point-of-entry systems treat water for the entire house where the main water line enters the house. Point-of-use filters clean water from the fixture to which they are attached.

Water Heating

Water heating can account for 14 to 25 percent of the energy consumed in your home. You can reduce your monthly water heating bills by selecting the appropriate water heater for your home or pool and by using some energy-efficient water heating strategies. If you plan to buy a new water heater, or replace an existing one, choose a system that will not only provide enough hot water but will also do so energy-efficiently, saving you money. Here's a quick look at the different kinds of water heating systems:

- **Conventional storage water heaters** The most popular type of water heating system for the home, these systems offer a ready reservoir—from 20 to 80 gallons—of hot water. Conventional storage water heater fuel sources include natural gas, propane, fuel oil and electricity. Because the water is constantly heated in the tank, energy can be wasted even when a hot water tap isn't running. You can find some storage water heater models with heavily insulated tanks, however, which significantly reduce standby heat losses,

Water Safety and Conservation Resources

- epa.gov/safewater and epa.gov/watersense; 800-426-4791 The EPA's water conservation and safety-related sites, and Safe Drinking Water Hotline.

- wateruseitwisely.com For 100 ways to conserve water in your area and info on how to contact your water authority.

- nsf.org National Sanitation Foundation, a not-for-profit, nongovernmental organization and provider of public health and safety risk management solutions, provides public health and safety-related information to concerned consumers around the world.

- apps1.eere.energy.gov/consumer/your_home/water_heating The DOE's Energy Efficiency and Renewable Energy site offers tips on lowering your water heating bills.

lowering annual operating costs. Look for models with tanks that have a thermal resistance (R-value) of R-12 to R-25.

- **Demand (tankless or instantaneous) water heaters** These systems provide hot water only as it is needed. They don't produce the standby energy losses associated with storage water heaters, which can save you money. Typically, demand water heaters provide hot water at a rate of 2 to 5 gallons per minute. Gas-fired demand water heaters produce higher flow rates than electric ones. For homes that use 41 gallons or less of hot water daily, demand water heaters can be 24 to 34 percent more energy-efficient than

You can lower the cost of heating your swimming pool by installing an energy-efficient pool heater, such as a heat pump or solar pool heaters, which can cost more than gas pool heaters, but have lower annual operating costs.

conventional storage tank water heaters. They can be 8 to 14 percent more energy efficient for homes that use a lot of hot water—around 86 gallons per day. You can achieve even greater energy savings of 27 to 50 percent if you install a demand water heater at each hot water outlet.

- **Heat pump water heaters** These systems use electricity to move heat from one place to another instead of generating heat directly to heat water. They can be either stand-alone water heating systems, or be a combination water-heating and space-conditioning system. You can also retrofit a heat pump to work with an existing conventional storage water heater. They can only be installed in locations that remain in the 40°–90°F range year-round and provide at least 1,000 cubic feet of air space around the water heater. Heat pump water heater systems typically have higher initial costs than conventional storage water heaters. However, they have lower operating costs, which can offset their higher purchase and installation prices.

- **Solar water heaters** Also called solar domestic hot water systems, these can be quite cost-effective in generating hot water for your home. They can also be used in any climate, and the fuel they use—sunshine—is free. Solar water heating systems include storage tanks and solar collectors. There are two types of solar water heating systems: active, which have circulating pumps and controls, and passive, which don't. Most solar water heaters require a well-insulated storage tank. Solar water heating systems almost always require a backup system for cloudy days and times of increased demand.

- **Tankless coil and indirect water heaters** These systems use a home's space-heating system to heat water. They're part of what's called integrated or combination water and space-heating systems.

Refrigerators and wine coolers use more energy than any other kitchen appliance, but Energy Star–approved models reduce energy consumption.

HOUSEHOLD APPLIANCES AND ELECTRONICS

In a typical U.S. home, appliances and home electronics— clothes washers and dryers, dishwashers, refrigerators and freezers, room air conditioners, water heaters, computers, TVs, DVD players and audio equipment—account for about 20 percent of the energy bills. A first step toward greening your home with respect to appliances and electronics is to choose and use no more than you really need. Next, be sure to choose the most energy-efficient appliance or home electronic item you can find.

Thanks to standards established by federal agencies charged with helping consumers purchase more energy-efficient products, there has been a marked improvement in appliance performance over the past several years. In addition to the Federal Trade Commission (FTC), these agencies include the previously mentioned Department of Energy (DOE) and the Environmental Protection Agency (EPA), which jointly run the country's Energy Star program. When shopping for and comparing energy-efficient

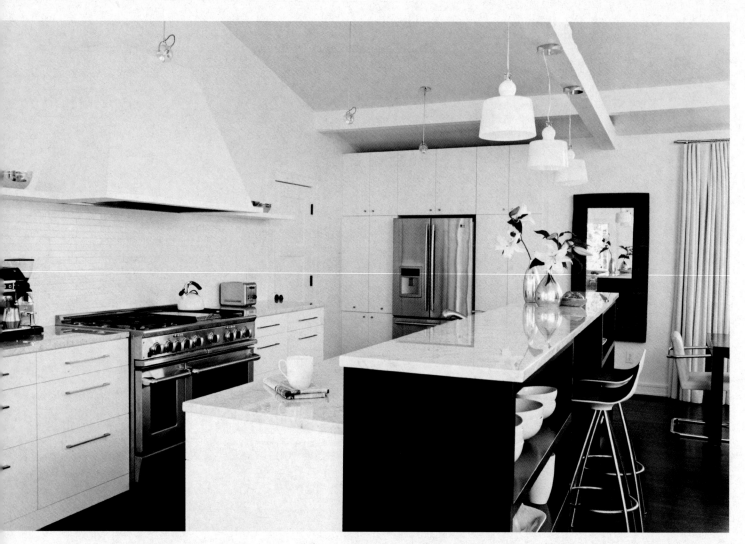

appliances, always look for the yellow and black Energy Guide label, which is required by the U.S. Federal Trade Commission on most home appliances, except for stove ranges and ovens. (The Energy Guide label is also not required on home electronics, such as computers, televisions and home audio equipment.) Energy Guide labels provide an estimate of the product's energy consumption or energy efficiency. They also show the highest and lowest energy consumption or efficiency estimates of similar appliance models.

Also look for Energy Star labels, which appear on appliances and home electronics that meet strict energy-efficiency criteria established by the DOE and EPA. The

Energy Star program labels most home electronics and appliances, except for water heaters, stove ranges and ovens, and helps consumers reduce their energy bills and greenhouse gas emissions. In some cases Energy Star–approved appliances cost 10 to 15 percent more than comparable products, but the savings in energy costs over their lifespan should more than cover this initial investment. Also, many local water and power companies offer rebates or tax incentives for replacing old appliances with new energy-efficient models. Contact your local utility, or enter your zip code under the rebate finder on the Energy Star website to find out about possible rebates (*see sidebar page 88*).

Calculating and Controlling Energy Efficiency

The DOE's Energy Efficiency and Renewable Energy website offers tools than can help you decide whether to invest in a more energy-efficient appliance, determine your electricity loads, or estimate appliance energy consumption. To estimate an appliance's energy consumption, for example, it offers this formula:

Wattage × Hours Used Per Day ÷ 1000 = Daily Kilowatt-hour (kWh) consumption.

You should multiply this by the number of days you use the appliance during the year for the annual consumption. You can then calculate the annual cost to run an appliance by multiplying the kWh per year by your local utility's rate per kWh consumed.

One caveat: To estimate the number of hours that a refrigerator actually operates at its maximum wattage, you'll need to divide the total time the refrigerator is plugged in by three. Although they are turned "on" all the time, refrigerators actually cycle on and off to maintain interior temperatures.

You can usually find the wattage of most appliances stamped on the bottom or back of the appliance, or on its nameplate. If the wattage is not listed on the appliance, you can still estimate it by finding the current draw (in amperes), which is typically printed on a rating plate attached to the appliance, and multiplying that by the voltage used by the appliance. Most appliances in the United States use 120 volts. Larger appliances, such as clothes dryers and electric cooktops, use 240 volts.

Many appliances continue to draw a small amount of power, known as a phantom load, when they are switched off. This occurs in most appliances that use electricity, such as televisions, stereos, computers and kitchen appliances. These loads can be eliminated by unplugging the appliance, or by using a power strip and switching off the power strip to cut all power to the appliance when it's not in use.

If you have an older appliance, you can also use a power-controlling device to reduce the energy consumption of the appliance's electric motor. These power-controlling devices basically regulate the power delivered to an appliance's motor by continuously adjusting the 60-cycle sine wave from the utility to match changes in the load on the motor. Appliances newer than 1990 may see no energy savings at all, due to their existing energy-saving features. In some cases, the controller slightly increases the appliance's electrical consumption.

Cooking Appliances

From an energy perspective, your refrigerator will be more important than your cooking appliances, since the fridge will operate around the clock. As a result, cooking appliances aren't even covered by the Energy Star program or the minimum federal efficiency standards. So if you want to choose a green cooking device you'll need to choose whether you want one that consumes less energy to cook or one that creates less indoor air pollution. Here's a brief summary of the characteristics of different types of cooking appliances.

- **Gas Cooktops** Gas appliances are certainly more energy-efficient than electric ones, and they burn the fuel where you need it. But burning gas produces potentially harmful combustion, with byproducts including carbon monoxide,

Opposite: A sleek range hood eliminates contaminants and blends seamlessly with a kitchen designed by Yianni Doulis and Jessica Helgerson.

Right: In a compact kitchen designed by Scott Martin of Blue Plum Design, a downdraft vent rises when needed from an island cooktop.

don't pollute your home with combustion byproducts. If you have a gas oven, you should run the exhaust fan while the oven is operating. Self-cleaning ovens usually are better insulated than manual ovens, making them more efficient.

- **Microwave Ovens** Heating though the use of high-frequency radio waves, microwaves reduce cooking time and energy use by up to 75 percent, making them extremely energy-efficient. But they are not suitable for certain types of cooking, such as browning and baking, so some people opt to forgo them. Others are concerned that they cause food to lose nutritional value or make food radioactive, despite a lack of any convincing evidence. And all manufacturers must comply with federal safety regulations to make them safe to operate.

carbon dioxide and nitrogen dioxide. If you cook with gas, always use a range hood, preferably one that is ducted to the outside. And look for gas ranges with sealed burners.

- **Electric Cooktops** Among the electric cooktops sold in the U.S., most have either coil elements or heat-resistant ceramic glass placed over radiant ribbons. Both offer similar efficiency, though coil elements heat up faster. Other electric cooktops include solid disk, halogen and induction burners. Solid disk and halogen technologies are less efficient or as efficient as coil or ceramic glass cooktops. But induction cooktops are the most energy-efficient of all electric technologies. They're also very responsive to temperature settings, almost comparable to gas ranges. However, they are very expensive.

- **Convection Ovens** Because these ovens have an internal fan that distributes hot air evenly, temperatures and cooking times can be decreased, reducing energy use by up to 30 percent. They're more expensive, however, and may not be worth the savings in your energy bill, unless you cook a lot.

- **Conventional Gas and Electric Ovens** Electric ovens maintain a more even temperature than gas ovens and they

Green Kitchen Tips

Be as healthy and energy-efficient as possible in the kitchen by following these tips:

- Eliminate the use of small electronic gadgets for chopping, grinding and mixing by handling these tasks manually instead.
- Install a carbon monoxide alarm.
- Cook meals in small appliances, such as a microwave or toaster oven, to save energy.
- Recycle your old appliances. Ask your power company about recycling rebates, check with your local recycling department or visit *earth911.org* to find out how to recycle appliances you plan to replace.
- Refrigerate responsibly and opt out of installing special wine, outdoor or mini-refrigerators if possible.
- Replace a refrigerator that is more than 12 years old with a new Energy Star–approved model.
- Choose a refrigerator with a freezer on top. It's more efficient than a bottom freezer model and much more efficient than a side-by-side model.
- Avoid refrigerators with through-the-door ice and water dispensers. They can increase energy consumption by up to 20 percent.
- Keep plates under burners clean so they reflect heat well.
- Check to be sure gas flames burn blue. If the flames are orange, your burners probably need servicing.

- **Range hoods:** Whether you choose an under-cabinet model, a chimney-style version, or a downdraft style, a range hood's primary job is to remove contaminants like carbon monoxide and eliminate odors. As such, the downdraft systems aren't as effective as the overhead models, and to really work properly they must be vented to the outdoors.

Home Electronics

From a green perspective, it's hard to find simple answers to simple questions about home electronics. Say, for example, you want to know whether LCD and plasma display TVs are more energy-efficient than old cathode ray tube (CRT) screens. Or you'd like to know which is more energy-efficient,

a plasma or LCD. The answer depends not only on which kind of flat screen you're talking about, but also on when you purchased or plan to purchase it, how big it is, how you use it and how power consumption is measured today.

In terms of the new flat-screen TVs versus old CRT TVs, for example, flat-screen TVs typically consume more energy than smaller-screened CRT TVs. One report found that plasma televisions, which are often about 50 percent bigger than their cathode-ray-tube equivalents, consume about four times

Opposite: A stainless steel range hood complements this kitchen's industrial-style light fixtures, which are fitted with energy-saving CFLs.

Above: A compact, under-counter refrigerator suffices for a family of two and requires a lot less energy to operate than a large one.

more energy. And when looking at the carbon emissions from the power plants, the same report found that old-style TVs produce about one-quarter of the climate-warming CO_2 per year that larger plasma screens do.

As far as the green trade-offs between plasma versus LCDs, the prevailing wisdom is that plasma screens are the bigger consumers of power because a plasma screen is made up of pixels, each of which has an individual light source that gets illuminated as needed. An LCD always has a backlight illuminating the entire screen. As a result, energy consumption also varies depending on what you're watching. A test conducted by *Call for Help*, a television program spotlighting technology, measured the electricity consumed by similar-sized plasma and LCD televisions. It found that most of the time LCD screens consumed less power, except when they displayed a solid color background on the screen or when there was static electricity.

Size also matters. The consensus seems to be that with smaller-screen TVs (under 40 inches), an LCD is generally more efficient than a CRT television. But for large screen sizes (50 inches and above), a projection TV may be the most efficient type of television you can buy.

You'll save electricity most of the time by buying an LCD though you'll spend more on the initial purchase. You'll also save power if you unplug it from the wall when you're not using it. These savings increase if you've got DVD players, tuners, and other systems hooked up to your TV, since they typically remain in a low-powered but standby mode when you shut them off as well. Plasma-screen TVs generate a lot of heat, use more current and require 60 percent more power than an equivalent LCD.

Home Office Efficiency

For the 18 million home-based business owners and some 24 million telecommuting Americans—as well as unemployed people searching for jobs through their PCs— higher energy bills for combined home offices and residences can eat away

at profits. But there are ways to reduce energy costs while taking care of business at home.

A lot of personal computers now come with a power-down or sleep mode feature for the CPU and monitor. Energy Star–rated computers power down to a sleep mode that consumes 15 watts of power or less—about 70 percent less than the electricity used by a computer without power management features. Energy Star–rated monitors can power down into two successive sleep modes, one more efficient than the other. To make the power-down feature effective,

Opposite: Light fixtures on dimmers, reflective surfaces, windows, and sleek draperies create an easy-to-control, energy-efficient lighting scheme.

Above: A mix of pendant, task and recessed ceiling fixtures are fitted with dimmable, energy-efficient light sources for layered illumination.

For more efficiency, be sure your monitors, printers and other accessories are on a power strip/surge protector. When this equipment is not in use for extended periods, turn off the switch on the power strip to prevent them from drawing power even when shut off. If you don't use a power strip, unplug extra equipment when it's not in use.

To cut related annual energy expenses by 30 percent, choose Energy Star–labeled computers, monitors, printers, scanners, copiers, fax machines, multi-function devices, lighting, cordless phones, answering machines, audio equipment and room air conditioners.

The quantity and quality of light in our home profoundly affects

A sculptural overhead fixture and compact desk lamp add energy-efficient function and style to this compact workspace.

however, you must activate it on your PC through your operating system software.

Also, be aware that screen savers are not energy savers—and in fact can use more energy than not using one. Plus, the power-down feature may not work if you have a screen saver activated. Modern LCD color monitors do not need screen savers at all.

As far as turning off your computer when it's not in use, bear in mind that though there is a small surge in energy when a computer starts up, this small amount of energy is still less than the energy used when a computer is running for long periods of time. For energy savings and convenience, turn off the monitor if you aren't going to use your computer for more than 20 minutes and turn off both the CPU and monitor if you're not going to use your computer for more than 2 hours.

Wattage of Standard Appliances and Electronics

Here are a few examples of the range of wattages for various household appliances:

Clock radio	=	10
Clothes washer	=	350–500
Clothes dryer	=	1,800–5,000
Coffeemaker	=	900–1,200
Dehumidifier	=	785
Dishwasher	=	1,200–2,400 (using the drying feature greatly increases energy consumption)
Ceiling fan	=	65–175
Whole-house fan	=	240–750
Hair dryer	=	1,200–1,875
Clothes iron	=	1,000–1,800
Microwave oven	=	750–1,100
Personal computer		
CPU (awake/asleep)	=	120 / 30 or less
Monitor (awake/asleep)	=	150 / 30 or less
Laptop	=	50
Radio (stereo)	=	70–400
Refrigerator (frost-free, 16 cubic feet)	=	725
Television (color)		
19"	=	65–110
36"	=	133
Flat screen	=	120
Toaster	=	800–1,400
VCR/DVD player	=	17–21/20–25
Vacuum cleaner	=	1,000–1,440
Water heater (40-gallon)	=	4,500–5,500

LIGHTING

our health, comfort and productivity. But artificial lighting also consumes energy—almost 15 percent of a household's electricity use. However, new fixtures, sources and lighting controls can reduce lighting energy use in homes by up to 75 percent. To reduce energy consumed by lighting, consider these illumination strategies for inside the house and out.

Indoors

Install fluorescent bulbs in all ceiling- and wall-mounted fixtures that will be on for more than 2 hours each day, and if possible, use dedicated compact fluorescent fixtures, rather than inserting CFL bulbs in incandescent fixtures, to ensure the use of fluorescents over the life of the house. Also, choose Energy Star–labled fixtures if possible and install occupancy sensors that will automatically turn lights on and off as needed.

Most energy-efficient light sources have color temperatures that generate a cooler light than incandescents. Also, their ability to render color in a way that's true varies considerably. However, advances in technology have enabled the color temperature or color rendering capability of some of these sources to more closely resemble that of incandescent sources or the quality of daylight. In general, cool light is preferable for visual tasks because it produces higher contrast than warm light. Warm light is better for living spaces because it is more flattering to skin tones and clothing.

Because most objects are not just one color but a combination of many colors, light sources that don't render color well may change the apparent color of an object. A bulb's Color Rendition Index (CRI) measures its ability to render colors the same way sunlight does. Ranked on a scale of 1 to 100, with 100 at the top, a CRI value of 100 is based on illumination by a 100-watt incandescent lightbulb. A light source with a CRI of 80 or higher is considered acceptable for most indoor residential applications.

Exterior lanterns flanking the door are fitted with energy-efficient sources to softly illuminate a covered patio on this home by Wesketch Architecture.

Outdoors

In residential settings, outdoor lighting illuminates the house and landscape, provides security and helps people navigate to and from the house. Security and utility lighting does not need to be bright to be effective, so efficient, lower-wattage light sources can do the trick. If possible, use fluorescent, high-intensity discharge (HID), or low-pressure sodium lights combined with motion sensors or photosensors. Also, choose fixtures that have reflectors or covers to make more efficient use of the light source and control light pollution. If possible, use timers or other controls to turn decorative lighting on and off, and install solar lighting whenever possible.

Daylighting

For the most efficient use of light in your home, it's helpful to combine your artificial lighting scheme with daylighting strategies, which are provided through windows and skylights and enable you to minimize the use of artificial light during the day. Maximize the use of natural daylight in your home to further reduce the need for artificial lighting. The best approach to daylighting in your home will depend on your climate and home's design. The sizes and locations of windows should be based on the cardinal directions rather than their effect on the street-side appearance of the house.

- **South-facing windows** are best for daylighting and for moderating seasonal temperatures, as they allow maximum winter sunlight into the home. You can minimize direct sun during the summer with proper shades.
- **North-facing windows** admit relatively even, natural light, producing little glare and almost no unwanted heat gain.
- **East- and west-facing windows** provide good daylight in the morning and evening, respectively, but should be limited, as the light they admit causes glare and heat during

Turning Off the Lights

The cost-effectiveness of turning off lights depends on the type of lights and the price of electricity. The type of light is important for several reasons. All types of light sources have a rated operating life. But the operating life of all types of lightbulbs depends on how many times they are turned on and off. The more often they are switched on and off, the lower their operating life.

- Incandescent bulbs should be turned off whenever they are not needed. Most incandescent lightbulbs are fairly inexpensive to produce and are relatively inefficient. Only about 10 to 15 percent of the electricity that incandescent lights consume results in light—the rest is turned into heat.
- Fluorescent lights are more complex to evaluate from a cost-effectiveness perspective when deciding whether to leave them on or turn them off. In most areas of the United States, a general rule of thumb is to turn them off if you leave a room for more than 15 minutes. Fluorescent lights are more expensive to buy, and their operating life is more affected by the number of times they are switched on and off, relative to incandescent lights.

Switching to a Green Power Provider

There is a difference between suppliers and deliverers of power. The former create electricity, while the latter maintain power lines and bring the electricity to your home. Consumers can only change power suppliers. Armed with this knowledge, here's how you can make the switch:

- Finding green power suppliers Check out Green-e (*green-e.org*), a group that allows people to search for companies that supply certified green power in their state. (The certification is done by the nonprofit Center for Resource Solutions, which annually verifies that the providers live up to the renewable-energy guidelines set by Green-e.) Go to "Buy Green-e Certified," select your state, and a handful of choices should pop up. In your area, these might include purveyors of hydropower, wind power or a combination of both. In addition to Green-e, you can go to the U.S. Department of Energy's Green Power Network site for a list of sustainable energy options offered in each state.
- Taking stock In order to choose the best (and least expensive) solution, dig out your electric bills and average the supply cost of your electricity over the last year. Look over your statements carefully to find just the supply cost—it can be hidden in the Notes section.
- Perusing plans Once you know your average cost—say 14.1¢ per kilowatt hour (kwh)—go to the website of each of the green power suppliers in your area and look at their different plans. Some have fixed-rate options (usually lasting one year), and some propose variable-rate plans, in which the cost fluctuates as the market does.
- Running the numbers Compare your 14.1¢ rate with the green plans that offer fixed rates. One such plan could cost 15.4¢ per kwh for mixed power (wind and hydro); another may cost 16.9¢ for all wind. Most companies offering variable-rate plans list on their websites what they have been charging for green power over the past several months. (If you find one that doesn't provide such information, make a call and ask.) Some of these companies can average cheaper rates than both your regular supplier and the green fixed-rate plans!
- Making a decision After comparing differences, you'll probably choose the one with the lowest average rate over the past several months, say a mixed-power variable-rate plan. Once you switch from fossil fuel–generated energy your bills will decrease. It feels pretty good to be green.

the summer when it is usually not wanted. They also contribute little to solar heating during the winter.

Solar Power

Flip a switch, and the lights turn on. Plug in a power cord, and electricity flows. Our household power needs are instantly met, and until recently, we've given little thought to the costs—both economic and environmental—of having electricity so readily available. But green awareness casts a different light on this everyday convenience. In the United States, electrical power is generated by facilities that rely on (in descending order) coal, natural gas or nuclear power—all sources that come with serious environmental caveats. As for

price, electricity is still relatively affordable, although the dollar amount varies by region (ranging from 5¢ per kilowatt hour in Wyoming to 16¢ per kilowatt hour in Connecticut). With the average American household use at 11,000 kilowatt-hours per year, the average annual residential electrical price tag comes in under $1,000—but costs are bound to increase as the environmental toll mounts.

One of the greenest things you can do is tap into the power of the sun for some or all of your home's electrical needs. Do you need to live in sunny California to take advantage of the sun's energy? Not at all. As long as a portion of your roof gets full sunlight between 10 A.M. and 2 P.M. year-round, you're a candidate for rooftop-mounted solar panels, which have improved vastly in both looks and technology in recent years. Whereas solar panels once were used almost exclusively for heating your home's water supply

A trio of stylish pendants provides dimmable focused illumination over the dining table, while ceiling fixtures on separate switches offer diffuse ambient light.

Choosing your Bulb

A "lamp" is the term used in the lighting industry to describe what is most commonly called a lightbulb. The key to lighting energy savings lies in your choice of lamps. Check out the options:

- **Traditional incandescent** The most frequently used lamps in residential applications, they provide a warm, consistent and diffuse light. They are inexpensive but not energy efficient. Average cost: 75¢ per bulb. They last about 750–2,500 hours. Their color temperature is about 2,700–2,800 degrees Kelvin.

- **Compact fluorescent** CFLs use ⅕ to ⅓ the electricity of an incandescent yet last up to 10 times longer without sacrificing the amount of light. These sources have a reputation for offering cool and diffuse light, but they've improved in recent years to provide a warmer light that resembles incandescent or natural light. Average cost: $2.50 per bulb. These lamps last up to 10,000 hours. The color temperature of warm-white CFLs is about 2,700–3,000 degrees Kelvin; cool-white or bright-light CFLs are 4,000–4,200 degrees Kelvin. Daylight CFLs are rated as 5,000 degrees Kelvin and higher.

- **Tungsten halogen** They produce a bright, warm incandescent light. They also have a longer life and are more energy-efficient than standard incandescent bulbs, but are not as efficient as CFLs. They usually provide focused light. Average cost: about $4 per bulb. Their color temperature ranges from 2,900–3,200 degrees Kelvin. They last about 2,000–4,000 hours.

- **Xenon and krypton** These incandescent sources produce clear, warm, white light and are very energy-efficient. Xenon bulbs come in a wide range of shapes and sizes with a variety of bases for different applications, including under-cabinet lighting. They last about 10,000 hours, with color temperatures from 3,000-12,000 degrees Kelvin. Average cost: about $4 per bulb.

- **LED** Light-emitting diode bulbs provide a bright, clear light, and professionals believe as technology improves, they will replace CFLs and incandescent bulbs. They are highly energy-efficient and last 50–100 times longer than a standard incandescent (up to 20 years), but their color rendering ability is still evolving. Color temperatures start at about 2,700 degrees Kelvin. They last between 30,000–100,000 hours. Average cost: $15–$100 per bulb.

(in the 1970s and '80s), today there are many applications of solar power—from providing your home's electricity to heating the swimming pool. Best of all, there are state and federal tax incentives and rebates that are making it more affordable for homeowners to follow their green conscience, reimbursing 25% or more of installation costs. Here's information to help you decide what's right for you.

While all these applications are popular, solar power is so site-specific—depending on your roof's orientation, size, shading, and other factors—that you will want to have a professional assess your home's potential. Use the "Find a Solar Pro" tool *atases.org* (the American Solar Energy Society) to get started. It's also helpful to become familiar with the incentives and rebates available where you live. A good clearinghouse of state-by-state information can be found at *dsireusa.org*, the Database of State Incentives for Renewables & Efficiency. Each state has its own energy office, which can be found through an Internet search, and there is good basic information about solar power at the U.S. Department of Energy's website, *eere.energy.gov*.

POWER THE WHOLE HOME: PHOTOVOLTAICS

Photovoltaic (PV) systems use an array of solar panels or modules to create electricity for a home; the rooftop-mounted panels are connected to the house's electrical panel, and the whole system can be tied into the power grid, meaning a homeowner can end up with a credit from the power company. New technology has resulted in PV cells that are sleek and unobtrusive, ranging from jet black to dark blue.

A photovoltaic system can be sized to meet your entire household's electrical needs or just a portion: a 5-kilowatt system of sleek polycrystalline PV cell modules, for example, might cover several hundred square feet of roof, at an installed cost (before rebates) of $40,000 to $50,000, and generate 5,500 kilowatt-hours per year.

SMALL-SCALE SOLAR POWER

If the initial cost of a large photovoltaic system is too high, or if the portion of your roof that gets full sun is small, you may consider a smaller photovoltaic system. For example, a 2-kilowatt array of modules could be installed on a garden shed roof, or south-facing porch roof, generating 2,000

kilowatt-hours per year. A typical roof-mounted grid-connected photovoltaic system costs between $7 to $9 per watt, making a 2kW photovoltaic stystem around $18,000 (before rebates). Note: The initial ticket price may be less for a smaller system; however, it costs more per watt than a larger system.

Solar-Powered Water Heater Using the sun's energy to preheat the water that goes into an existing hot water heater reduces the energy outlay needed before domestic hot water is delivered to the shower, sink or laundry. A typical system might include two 4 x 8-foot flat plate collectors mounted on the roof, and an 80- to 120-gallon storage tank; installed costs run from $10,000 to $15,000 (before rebates).

Solar Pool Heating Rooftop-mounted collection equipment allows the sun to heat your pool water, eliminating the need for a conventional pool heater. Rooftop tubes or plates—typically mounted on a poolhouse or outbuilding near the pool—receive water from your tap, the sun heats the water, then the water is sent to the pool itself. The cost runs about $4,500 to $6,000 installed (before rebates).

Large picture windows in a living space designed by architect Joseph Eisner let in natural light and open onto views of the pool and wooded surroundings. Energy-efficient recessed ceiling fixtures provide ambient light at night, while a pendant provides task illumination next to the reading chair.

What's Inside?

Surrounding yourself with an eco-friendly landscape and building a healthy, well-insulated home powered with energy-efficient systems and appliances are essential first steps toward green living. But the surfaces inside your home—the walls, floors, cabinets and countertops—are equally important ingredients in a nurturing, sustainable household. Because you'll come into contact with these surfaces on a daily basis, they should be as comforting and environmentally friendly as possible. Unfortunately, many of these elements can be made of materials or treated with finishes that can do more harm than good—particularly in newer homes with tighter building envelopes, which can seal in toxic emissions that deteriorate indoor air quality.

Thanks to the growing demand for environmentally friendly building products, however, healthier, nonpolluting surfaces and finishes are now becoming readily available in the market and are competitive in cost and performance to comparable, more toxic products. And as with exterior materials, the options are vast and their eco-friendliness is variable. So from a green perspective, you'll sometimes have to make tradeoffs between durability, healthy materials, aesthetics and price. The following overview of interior surface options will provide ideas on choices that can nurture and support your health and the planet's, too.

Previous page: White-washed brick and rusticated wood beams add eco-friendly character to a room furnished by designer Janie Hirsch.

Above: In the living room of a home designed by Wesketch Architecture, sustainable wood floors and ceiling trusses add warmth.

- **Gypsum** If you haven't opted for one of the earth-masonry construction methods for your home, and it has been built with a frame construction, the interior walls will likely be made of gypsum board, which is also known as drywall or Sheetrock. Composed of natural gypsum sandwiched between smooth paper surfaces made of recycled newsprint, the 4 x 8-foot sheets are attached to a home's framing studs, then taped, sealed and textured or painted. They are predisposed to mold growth if exposed to water damage, and the joint compound used to cover the seams between them may contain toxic chemicals. They can also absorb toxic byproducts of combustion that can outgas into the building envelope. To control these issues, gypsum board should be tightly sealed and taped, treated with a low-toxicity powdered joint cement or texture compound, and have foamed or gasketed sills and top plates around all openings, such as windows and doors, to limit moisture penetration. Other options include glass-faced wallboards or magnesium oxide boards, which are most resistant to mold and moisture. Also, moisture-resistant cementitious backerboards without paper backings or like surfaces should be used in areas such as tub and shower surrounds.

- **Plaster** While expensive due to the labor involved in its application, plaster is both a beautiful and healthy interior wall finish. It's good at blocking trace amounts of VOCs in gypsum board, but, due to shrinkage or shifting, can develop cracks, which should be filled with a nontoxic sealant. Plasters that contain polyvinyl additives that can outgas should be avoided. Because of their good hygroscopic qualities, clay-based plasters are wonderful interior wall finishes. But plasters are porous and will show stains unless properly finished. You can apply a natural finish, such as beeswax, over plaster. Or you can protect the surface with paint or a synthetic clear finish, but be sure to evaluate these for toxic chemical contents to avoid problems with outgassing.

- **Paneling, Molding, Millwork & Trim** Eco-friendly wall paneling, molding and other architectural elements, such as

bead board, board and batten, wainscoting, crown molding, chair rails, columns and various trims that are made of wood or wood byproducts (including particleboard, MDF, veneer, solid lumber, hybrid lumber and other wood fiber products), should be certified by a recognized third-party verifier, such as the Forest Stewardship Council or SFI, Inc. When systems made with any of these kinds of wood products are marked with their seals, you'll know that they come from responsibly-managed forests. If you purchase a product containing wood byproducts, such as particleboard, which can contain high levels of formaldehyde, it's helpful to try to get a sense of the chemicals and adhesives used to make it. Choose a product that is manufactured with environmentally responsible practices that minimize waste and toxic additives. Many of these products are available preprimed or prepainted. Unless they're treated with a low- or no-VOC primer or paint, you

Low-VOC paint, bamboo flooring with a tile inset, and recycled pieces add interest to a kitchen by the Breakfast Room.

might want to opt for the unfinished variety, even though it will require extra finish work. Another green option is to use reclaimed lumber products salvaged from other architectural locations. Millwork and molding products are also available in synthetic materials, such as PVC, which are affordable, durable and easy to care for, but these will outgas toxic emissions. Because these products are lightweight, they can also be installed with adhesives, which often contain harmful chemicals. So if you or a family member have chemical sensitivities, it's best to avoid this option.

- **Stone, Tile & Grout** Since stone and tile are essentially inert materials, especially factory-finished tile that requires no further onsite finishing, they are considered healthy, eco-friendly wall surface materials. They are also long-lasting, low-maintenance materials. But if they come on some kind of synthetic backing, you'll need to be aware of the toxic emissions the backing might produce. Also, certain imported tiles are finished with lead-based or radioactive glazes, and sealing products for tiles can contain high levels of VOCs. Some green designers express concerns

about radon or radiation levels in stone and recommend that any stone, particularly granite, be screened for radon prior to installation. Stone and tile adhesives, mortars and grouts can also contain toxic chemicals, and some grouts contain additives or fungicides that can be harmful. Experts representing the International Institute for Bau-Biologie & Ecology, an organization dedicated to providing information on healthy, sustainable design, recommend installing tiles with a thickset method, using additive-free Portland cement, or a water-mixed thinset technique without synthetic additives if possible. While less toxic, these methods can be more prone to cracking, so for greater durability you'd need to use a water-mixed thinset with vinyl polymers. If you opt to use a tile adhesive, also known as an organic mastic, opt for a water-based product, such as AFM Safecoat 3-in-1 Adhesive. Use grouts without latex additives, if possible, and tile and grout sealers, such as AFM products, that are as free from harmful chemicals as possible.

- **Paints** Paint is the most common finish used on interior walls, but it can also be one of the primary perpetrators of indoor air pollution. Although the oil-based, or alkyd, paints that were frequently used for interior applications in the past are the more serious offenders due to the solvents

Architect Joseph Eisner placed leather bolsters into a wall made of certified mahogany to create a sculptural headboard.

they contain, these paints are rarely used in residential settings anymore, thanks to advances in the technology and durability of latex, or water-based, paints. While the range in toxicity and performance characteristics of latex paints is vast, numerous low- or no-VOC paints have recently become widely available. Keep in mind that VOC levels are typically expressed in grams per liter, or g/l. Until 1999, the VOC content in paints was pushing 1000 g/l, but federal regulations have since set the VOC content limit in paint at 250 g/l. To easily identify low- or no-VOC paints, look for products that feature a Green Seal sticker, the mark of approval of Green Seal, an independent group that sets standards for eco-conscious goods. The Green Seal certifies

interior paints as low VOC if the content is below 50 g/l for flat-coat or 150 g/l for non–flat-coat paints. Zero-VOC paints are paints that have a VOC content of 5 g/l or less.

PERFORMANCE AND PRICE

Eco-friendly paints were initially seen as a trend, but thanks to growing awareness of environmental issues, increased consumer demand and state initiatives to create stringent regulations, they are now acknowledged as permanent fixtures in the home decor industry. In fact, most leading

Left: The cabinetry in this bath is made of Lyptus, a wood product manufactured from two species of fast-growing, sustainable eucalyptus.

Above: Benjamin Moore's new eco-friendly Natura is a virtually odorless, zero-VOC paint that doesn't sacrifice style or performance.

What are VOCs?

If being in a freshly painted room gives you a sore throat, itchy eyes or a headache, you may be reacting to the volatile organic compounds (VOCs) in the solvents added to many commercial paints to give them their consistency. As the paint dries, the VOCs release gases. Exposure to these gases can be especially difficult for environmentally sensitive people or asthma sufferers, and long-term exposure can cause health problems.

Many paint manufacturers offer low- or no-VOC alternatives, including Behr's low-VOC paint, Benjamin Moore's Aura and Natura lines, Glidden's Evermore and Sherwin-Williams' GreenSure paints. A Green Seal label indicates that the paint contains a VOC level well below the Environmental Protection Agency's standard.

VOCs also outgas from stains, adhesives and synthetic flooring. VOCs may include carcinogenic chemicals, such as acetone, toluene, xylene, formaldehyde, and benzenes. According to the American Lung Association, these chemicals can be detected through symptoms such as eye, nose and throat irritation, headaches, skin irritation and fatigue. Coughing or shortness of breath can also signal the presence of VOCs.

paint manufacturers, including Pittsburgh Paints, Sherwin-Williams, DuPont, Benjamin Moore and American Pride, have lines of green paints. Even The Home Depot has a low-VOC paint with Glidden's Eco Options line. While many eco-friendly paints were at one time seen as synonymous with compromised quality and durability, new formulations perform as well as or even surpass their toxic counterparts. The eco-friendly paints do tend to be more expensive than conventional paints, however, with the price tag for low-VOC paint usually about $2 to $3 more per gallon. But demand is closing the price gap. Because they have fewer solvents and the conventional drying and curing agents have been removed (or reduced), they take longer to set and can be more difficult for inexperienced painters to apply. Among some of the other eco-friendly paints preferred by green designers are Enviro-Pure and Benjamin Moore's Aura and Natura, which are Green Seal–certified, and the various BioShield paints.

Durable, easy-to-clean black tile serves as wainscoting beneath a graphic nature-inspired wallpaper in this renovated powder room by Yianni Doulis and Jessica Helgerson. The countertops are Calacatta marble.

MILK PAINT

In use for hundreds of years, milk paint—paint made with milk protein, lime and natural pigments—is another green option. It gives rather sheer coverage, and until recently has been mainly used in restoration work or to give a weathered look to furniture. But because it's so environmentally friendly, it's being used more and more for walls. It is nontoxic, and odorless when dry, but can sour in its liquid form, and is not recommended for damp locations since it is susceptible to mildew.

- **Stains and Sealers** Since solvent-based wood stains and sealers can be highly toxic and outgas long after they've been applied to a wood surface, green designers recommend using water-based stains and finishes (such as BioShield or AgriStain), or bio-based stains that can be used on wood and painted surfaces. Other more healthful natural finishes include plant-based oils, lacquers, waxes and shellacs.

- **Wallcoverings** Although wallcovering manufacturers are jumping on the green bandwagon and beginning to produce eco-friendly products, many wallcoverings are vinyl-coated or are paper-backed vinyl, which contain VOCs that damage indoor air quality. They can also trap water vapors and produce mold. In addition, wallcoverings are typically applied with toxic adhesives, and the inks used to create their patterns can also contain harmful chemicals. If you want to use a wallcovering in a green home, search for one made with natural materials that can be applied with low-toxicity adhesive.

Paint Tips

- For a clean, sophisticated look on walls, choose paint in what is known as full-spectrum color, meaning a complex hue containing a mix of red, blue and yellow but no black. According to Michelle Quaranta, a C2 Paint color expert and owner of Colori, an eco-friendly paint boutique in Chicago, these hues have become popular because they blend with each other easily and are more luminous.

- To inhibit the growth of mold and mildew, look for anti-microbial paints, which wrap rooms in a layer of protection.

Ceiling SOS

From both an aesthetic and a green point of view, some ceilings that were popular 40 or 50 years ago should be replaced today.

- Popcorn Ceilings In the 1970s contractors bypassed the labor involved in creating smooth or hand surface-textured ceilings and saved money by using a spray-on technique to create what is commonly referred to as a "popcorn ceiling." With smooth or surface-textured ceilings preferred today, rooms with popcorn ceilings are typically viewed as eyesores by homeowners and potential buyers alike. If you've got a room with one of these ceilings and want to change it, your best bet is to call a professional. Since some of these ceilings contain asbestos, the job can be hazardous as well as difficult. Or, if you want information on how to safely remove such a ceiling, visit *naturalhandyman.com/iip/infpai/popcornoff.html*.

- Acoustical tile ceilings If you have a ceiling that's been covered up with acoustical ceiling tiles, consider covering the tiles with a flat surface and finishing it with plaster. You can also remove the tile and the furring strips attached to the lath and plaster ceiling, and install drywall directly against the ceiling. But because with old tile you need to be concerned about the presence of asbestos, you should call a professional to cut a sample and send it to an independent laboratory for analysis (look for "Asbestos Consulting & Testing" in the yellow pages). If the sample tests positive, have the tile removed by enlisting a contractor who specializes in asbestos removal. They can be found in the yellow pages under "Asbestos Abatement." Or contact the air-pollution-control authority in your area. They can provide information about asbestos abatement for homeowners who want to do the work themselves.

Cabinets

When you consider the fact that cabinets can eat up roughly half of a kitchen remodeling budget—according to the National Kitchen & Bath Association, a trade group that trains and certifies kitchen designers—the last thing you want them to do is degrade your indoor air quality. But since cabinets are often composed of materials that contain urea-formaldehyde, which causes a wide range of adverse health effects, including headaches; skin rashes; burning and itchy eyes, nose and throat; nausea and even possibly cancer, according to the U.S. EPA, they are in fact one of the worst contributors to indoor air pollution in the home. Nowadays, cabinet boxes or shells are rarely made of solid wood. Instead, they're typically constructed of interior-grade plywood or pressed-wood products, such as particleboard or MDF, most of which are made with formaldehyde as a binder. Although manufacturers have reduced emissions in pressed-wood products by 80 to 90 percent over the past 25 years or so, and emissions drop off considerably a few months after installation, some products can continue to outgas for years.

Cabinet interiors are sometimes thermally fused with a thin plastic resin called melamine, which helps prevent

formaldehyde from evaporating from the pressed wood. But if the melamine doesn't cover the entire surface or small holes are drilled along the edges, evaporation can still occur. Furthermore, cabinets can be treated with harmful solvent-based stains and finishes, which also contribute to the degradation of indoor air quality.

GREEN CHOICES

Because the materials and finishes and ways in which they are constructed are so variable, and because they can be standard or custom, and range from relatively inexpensive to extremely costly, the greenest choice you can make for cabinets will invariably involve a trade-off in one way or another. Consider the following eco-friendly options.

- **Recycle or revamp existing cabinets** The eco-friendliest choice you can make is to continue using your existing cabinets. If you've got wood cabinets with a worn finish, you can give them a lift by refinishing them with a low- or no-VOC paint. If you're handy, you can do this yourself, though it requires a fair amount of elbow grease. Cabinet repair companies can also reface wood veneer or laminate cabinets. If the layout of your kitchen works for you, you can

also upgrade cabinets by replacing just the doors. Another way to minimize impact on the environment is to look for salvaged cabinets or make cabinets out of reclaimed wood, though these choices will limit your aesthetic control.

- **Choose sustainably forested wood or wood-byproduct cabinets** According to the National Kitchen & Bath Association, wood is the number-one choice for cabinets in this country. If you opt for solid wood cabinets or cabinets with wood veneers, choose those made with woods certified by the Forest Stewardship Council or SFI, Inc., which are respected third-party organizations that evaluate wood products manufacturers for their forestry and environmentally safe manufacturing practices. Also look for cabinets made from FSC-certified particleboard or Medite II, a formaldehyde-free recycled wood fiber product made by SierraPine, rather than conventional MDF. Marine-grade plywood and plywood made with soy-based adhesive are other eco-friendly options, as is a product called Allowood,

Opposite: Architect Rick Renner's kitchen features counters made from recycled paper, bamboo cabinets, and cabinet pulls crafted from the building's old metal window sashes.

In the living space beyond, low-VOC paint covers the walls, and floors are sustainably harvested Maine birch. Right: Reclaimed wood floors and beams add warmth to a new kitchen.

Eco-Wise Wood Cabinets

Wood's beauty and great environmental life-cycle and construction characteristics make it one of the most environmentally friendly cabinet materials. Wood production consumes less energy, emits fewer greenhouse gases, releases fewer pollutants into the air and generates less water pollution than steel and concrete production, for example. Furthermore, trees absorb carbon dioxide from the atmosphere as they grow, enabling them to naturally reduce greenhouse gases and improve air quality.

If you buy woods that are certified by the Forest Stewardship Council or other respected third-party certification bodies, you'll know your purchase has not contributed to the destruction of the world's forests. For more information on green-certified woods, visit these sites:

- **fsc.org** The Forest Stewardship Council, the country's most well-regarded wood certification body, certifies sustainably harvested wood or wood-based products and provides information on such products and where they're available.

- **sfiprogram.org** Sustainable Forestry Initiative, Inc., an independent, charitable organization dedicated to promoting sustainable forest management, has created a forest certification standards and certification program that is used widely across North America. Its certified products are recognized by many leading green building rating programs in the United States, Canada and overseas, including the National Association of Home Builders and Green Globes.

- **greencabinetsource.org** The Kitchen Cabinet Manufacturers Association lists cabinet manufacturers who have been certified by its Environmental Stewardship Program (ESP). It is the only environmental certification program that specifically focuses on kitchen and bath cabinets, and certification is awarded based on compliance in five categories: air quality, product resource management, process resource management, environmental stewardship and community relations.

which is a hardwood lumber substitute made from faster-growing softwoods and agri-based materials.

- **Consider eco-friendly wood alternatives** Some cabinets are now made with a product called wheatboard, which is a compressed straw fiber product made without formaldehyde binders. Another eco-friendly non-wood option is bamboo, which looks like wood, but is actually a rapidly renewable grass that can be sustainably harvested. You might also consider metal cabinets, which, while conductive to electromagnetism, do not outgas. They can also be made from recycled content and are usually recyclable themselves.

- **Think twice about cabinets faced with laminates or vinyl** Although laminates may be made from recycled materials, they, like vinyl surfaces made of PVC, which outgases, are typically attached to particleboard boxes with glues, both of which typically contain harmful chemicals. As such, these products aren't recommended from a green perspective.

Above: Sustainable wide-plank wood floors bring warmth to an expansive kitchen with a vaulted ceiling. Opposite, top right: In this U-shaped kitchen, the pass-through room divider is clad in Lyptus, a sustainable material made from eucalyptus. The backsplash is glass tile, while the countertops are dark green polished stone and floors are refinished oak. Opposite, top left and bottom: Solid surface and engineered stone materials are durable and come in a wide range of colors and patterns.

• **Avoid exotic woods** Do not choose cabinets made from tropical or exotic hardwoods, especially zebrawood and ebony, unless they are FSC-certified. A lack of control in overseas forests and the energy involved in transporting these products don't make them wise green choices. You could opt, however, for cabinets made from reclaimed woods, such as teak, mahogany, ipe or rubberwood.

Counters

From a green point of view, a good counter surface is nonporous, stain- and scratch-resistant, locally produced, nontoxic and beautiful. None of the counter surface materials currently available in the market meet all of these criteria, however. So, as with most materials, you'll have to weigh the benefits of each of the options against the drawbacks before settling on the best choice for you. The countertop comparison that follows can help you sort through the pros and cons.

SOLID SHEET GRANITE

Pros Granite comes in a wide variety of beautiful colors and patterns and is very hard, making it extremely scratch- and stain-resistant. It also holds up to heat and looks substantial.

Cons It is very expensive and requires maintenance with periodic sealing with an impregnating finish. It absorbs oil and butter stains, and can crack.

Eco-Notes It is not renewable, and once it is removed from the earth it cannot be easily reused. It should also be tested for radon or radioactivity before installation. Look for a local source to reduce energy expended in transportation, seek out remnant slabs and finish with a low-VOC sealant.

ENGINEERED STONE

Pros Composed of quartz particles and resin, it is available in a larger range of colors than granite and has a nonporous surface that resists scratches, stains and heat. It's hygienic, easy to maintain and does not require sealing. (Brands on the market include Silestone, Caesarstone, DuPont Zodiaq, and Cambria Quartz.)

Cons It is heavy and expensive, and requires professional installation.

Eco-Notes The mining of the quartz impacts the environment, but it is safe and hygienic.

SOLID SURFACES

Pros Made by such companies as Avonite, DuPont (Corian), and Swanstone, nonporous solid-surface countertops are custom-made to your specifications and come in a rainbow of colors and patterns. They're seamless, stain-resistant, and scratches can be sanded out.

Cons These surfaces are vulnerable to hot pans, which can damage them. They can range from moderately expensive to more expensive than granite or marble. They're made from synthetic acrylics or polyesters.

Eco-Notes These products are durable.

CERAMIC TILE

Pros Ceramic tile is often inexpensive, durable and easy to clean. Because it's installed a section at a time, it can also be installed by a resourceful do-it-yourselfer. It is heatproof, stain- and water-resistant, and comes in a wide range of prices, colors, textures and designs.

Cons Tiles can easily chip or crack, grout lines become stained and custom-designed tiles are very expensive. Also, they result in countertops that aren't completely smooth and that can be uneven.

Eco-Notes Be sure to use nontoxic grouts and adhesives. Tile is generally inert and biodegradable, but some tiles are finished with glazes that contain elements that can be harmful to human health.

LAMINATES

Pros Made of paper raw materials, laminates are low-cost and have smooth surfaces that are easy to clean. They are also available in a wide range of colors and are inexpensive. (Brands include Formica, Nevamar and Wilsonart.)

Cons Scratches and chips are almost impossible to repair and seams show. Laminates also are finished with petrochemical-based resin.

Eco-Notes Resins used may include urea-formaldehyde. Look for laminates that advertise that formaldehyde is not used in their production. Adhesives used to bind the product to a particleboard surface can be toxic. Particleboard, interior-grade plywood and MDF substrates can outgas formaldehyde, unless FSC-certified. If you choose a laminate, get one that is Greenguard-certified.

Top: This bath is clad in an engineered quartz tile and the countertop is CaesarStone.

Above: White subway tile and marble counters contribute to the clean quality of this inviting kitchen.

WOOD OR BUTCHER BLOCK

Pros Priced low to high, wood countertops are warm and beautiful and come in a wide range of colors and finishes. Hardwoods, such as maple and oak, are most common. They are easy to clean and can be sanded and resealed as needed.

Cons Their porous surface can harbor mold growth and stains easily. It can also be damaged by water and heat. Scratches must be oiled or sealed according to manufacturer's instructions.

Eco-Notes Wood is a renewable resource. Look for wood with FSC certification. Finish wood counters with an odorless, nontoxic oil, such as walnut oil, and use solvent- and formaldehyde-free adhesives.

STAINLESS STEEL

Pros This nonporous, nonstaining surface is easy to clean and offers a sleek, industrial look for contemporary kitchens. It is also heat resistant and durable.

Cons It is expensive, noisy and may dent. You can't cut foods on a steel surface, and it conducts electricity, so proper ground fault interrupters are required to prevent possible electrocution.

Eco-Notes Mining for materials and the fabrication process required to make steel uses a large amount of energy and pollutes the environment. But it is often made of recycled content and can be recycled when it is no longer of use.

Above, left and right: Butcher block and recycled concrete and glass offer distinctive eco-friendly countertop options.

STONE

Pros Stones, such as marble, granite, slate and soapstone, are beautiful, durable, heatproof and waterproof. Often seen in historical as well as modern homes, soapstone has a rich, deep gray color, is smooth to the touch and somewhat stain-resistant. Slate is nonporous and nonstaining.

Cons Stone countertops are expensive, and marble is porous and stains easily unless professionally sealed. It can also scratch and may need periodic resealing. Soapstone requires regular maintenance with applications of mineral oil, and may crack and darken over time. Both soapstone and slate are softer than granite and can chip over time.

Eco-Notes The mining of any stone has a negative impact on the environment, as all are finite resources. Purchase salvaged stone if possible or buy stone products mined from within a 500-mile radius from fair-trade merchants. Stone should be tested for radon or radioactivity before installation.

COMPOSITE AND RECYCLED MATERIALS

Pros Composite and recycled materials offer interesting aesthetic alternatives. Some are made from recycled paper and combined with resins to form a hard surface that is warmer than stone, and others are made from recycled glass, granite or other aggregates and are held together with either cement or resin to make a terrazzo-like surface.

Cons Durability and stain resistance varies depending on the product.

Eco-Notes Their recycled content makes them appealing to green designers, but unless they have some accredited green certification, they can be difficult to judge from an environmental perspective. Look for low-VOC resin usage and, in the case of paper products, FSC certification.

Counter Surface Resources

A few of the companies producing eco-friendly counter surface products made from recycled paper and phenolic resin, or products made from recycled glass, cement and plastics include:

- Coverings, Etc., makers of Eco-Terr, at *coveringsetc.com*
- EnviroGLAS at *enviroglasproducts.com*
- IceStone at *icestone.biz*
- PaperStone at *paperstoneproducts.com*
- Richlite at *richlite.com*
- Squak Mountain Stone at *squakmountainstone.com*
- Trespa at *trespa.com*
- Vetrazzo at *vetrazzo.com*

Natural stone counters are beautiful, but some green designers cite concerns that granite and other stone surfaces can contain dangerous levels of radon, a colorless, odorless, radioactive gas that comes from the decay of uranium in soil and rocks.

You can get an inexpensive testing kit at hardware stores or online sources. If you use one of these kits and it shows elevated levels from your home's surfaces, you should have an independent certified testing lab conduct another test to pinpoint the source. For more info, go to *epa.gov/radon* or call the National Radon Information Hotline at 800-SOS-RADON.

Another source for information on various environmentally friendly surfaces and other household products is The Greenguard Environmental Institute (GEI). It is an industry-independent, nonprofit organization that oversees the Greenguard Certification Program, and its mission is to improve public health and quality of life through programs that improve indoor air. Visit its site at *greenguard.org*.

Above: Cabinets made from FSC-certified wood and topped with a low-VOC finish add eco-friendly chararacter to this kitchen.

Opposite: Bamboo flooring adds eco-friendly warmth to a bathroom designed for the Twin Maples show house in New Jersey.

FLOORING

According to the World Floor Covering Association, green flooring includes any flooring that is sustainable, recyclable or contains recycled content, leaves a small carbon footprint, or has low levels of VOCs (volatile organic compounds). As with most materials, different flooring types offer different degrees of environmental friendliness. Stone, for example, is durable but is nonrenewable and requires considerable energy to quarry, finish, transport and install. Carpet, on the other hand, is soft and absorbs sound, but it is not incredibly durable in general and attracts dirt and dust.

Since floors account for the largest surface area in your home apart from the walls, they'll have a major impact on indoor air quality. Aside from the raw material required to produce various flooring materials, the glues, finishes, adhesives and cleaners that are required to install and maintain them also present associated environmental impacts. To help you select flooring materials that will help you enhance your indoor air quality while minimizing environmental impact, the following summary highlights some of the primary characteristics of various common floor materials.

BAMBOO

While many people think of bamboo as a wood, it is actually the world's largest growing grass. It is a rapidly renewable resource that matures in three to five years. Though widely regarded as an eco-friendly choice because of its ability to quickly regenerate, bamboo usually isn't certified as meeting various environmental production or preservation standards. So try to learn as much as you can about the bamboo you are interested in before purchasing it. Most bamboo flooring comes from Asia, particularly China and Vietnam, making the energy expenditure and air emissions in the transportation to North America significant concerns.

While some adhesives used in bamboo flooring sometimes contain a urea-formaldehyde resin, other bamboo products containing minimal or no formaldehyde are also available. Bamboo flooring is hard, more so than many hardwoods, in fact, and can last from 30 to 50 years. It will also

biodegrade in landfills after it is removed or it can be burned for energy. It ranges from $4 to $8 per square foot.

STONE

Stone is a nonrenewable natural product that's durable and easy to maintain. According to the World Floor Covering Association, there is no generally accepted data on the environmental impacts of using stone as flooring. But it is recyclable and can be reclaimed, quarried and manufactured using best practices. Although stone is minimally processed, quarrying, cutting and polishing this heavy material requires a great deal of energy. Quarrying can also impact the surrounding landscape and water tables. And popular types of stone, such as granite, marble, sandstone, slate, soapstone and limestone, sometimes need to be transported long distances, also demanding a great deal of energy.

Potential radon emissions can be an issue with stone. To finish stone flooring, choose a low-VOC sealer—or select stone flooring that does not require sealing. Stone flooring can endure for centuries and can be disposed of safely or crushed and reused as aggregate for other building materials. Its price generally ranges from $3 to $10 per square foot.

CORK

Cork is a unique renewable resource in that only the bark is harvested without damaging or destroying the tree. According to the WFCA, cork floors are made from the waste of cork used to make wine stoppers, and a law passed in the U.S. in the 1930s called "The 9 Year Law" keeps cork from being harvested any sooner than every 9 years. To keep cork floors as green as possible, finish and install them with water-based finishes and adhesives.

If possible, choose all-natural cork flooring over cork-vinyl composites that have PVC backing. Cork flooring preserves its shape well and naturally resists mold and moisture. It's also durable, biodegradable and nontoxic. It costs about $3 to $6 per square foot.

CERAMIC AND GLASS TILE

Used as flooring for thousands of years, ceramic tile is durable, rarely releases emissions, requires little maintenance, and can contain recycled content from lightbulbs, ground glass and other materials. It is also made from abundant natural clays. But its weight demands the use of more fuel for transportation than other products, so choose tile from a local source to reduce energy consumption. In terms of indoor air quality, consider setting ceramic tile in cement rather than using adhesives. If tiles are glazed, they are highly moisture- and stain-resistant. If unglazed, they are more porous and not as smooth to the touch. Ceramic tile biodegrades after removal. Tiles can be reused and may also be crushed and recycled as aggregate materials. Generally, it costs between $1 to $6 per square foot.

HARDWOOD

Hardwood is a wonderful green floor choice because it is natural, renewable, durable and recyclable. To be sure your hardwood is as green as possible, choose either reclaimed or salvaged wood floors from another site, or be sure new wood flooring is certified as environmentally friendly by an accredited certifier, such as the Forest Stewardship Council (FSC), Scientific Certification Systems (SCS), the American Tree Farm System (ATFS), or the Sustainable Forestry Initiative (SFI), all trusted organizations that certify that wood is grown and harvested from specially managed forests. Hardwood flooring certified as environmentally friendly by these organizations ensures that the wood is not clear cut, a forestry/logging practice in which most or all trees in a forest sector are cut down, but is instead harvested in a sustainable fashion. According to the WFCA, only 4 percent of the nation's native, old-growth forests are still standing. The U.S. is the world's largest importer and consumer of timber wood and wood products. Virgin hardwood flooring should be harvested from trees with long growth cycles, including red and white oak, maple, ash or birch. Avoid hardwoods that are exotic, rare or endangered. Some hardwood flooring is engineered, meaning that instead of solid hardwood, it is made of several wood layers of material with a hardwood veneer. If you choose an engineered wood, opt for a certified floor, as the substrates of engineered wood floors are often made of wood byproducts bonded with substances that can contain toxic elements. You can buy wood flooring that's been prefinished at the factory, where outgassing can be handled in a controlled environment. Or you can get it unfinished. Wood itself outgases minimally and does not harbor dust mites or mold. But wood floors require sealing, so choose sealers that give off few or no VOCs. Engineered and solid wood floors usually range from $3 to $6 per square foot.

LAMINATE

Laminate flooring is a versatile, durable, attractive flooring with the appearance of a hardwood, tile or stone floor. Although wood-look laminate flooring looks like solid wood, there is actually no solid wood used in its construction. Laminate floors are made up of several layers of materials, often including a moisture-resistant layer under a layer of HDF (high-density fiberboard) and topped with a high-resolution photographic image of natural wood flooring. These are bonded together under high pressure. The flooring is then finished with an extremely hard, clear coating made from special resin coated cellulose to protect the surface. Makers of laminate flooring argue that it is environmentally friendly as it uses less wood in its construction than solid wood or engineered wood floors, and it makes more efficient use of the wood fiber, sawdust or wood chips that are used as its substrate. But it may also contain formaldehyde or other toxic substances. Look for a FloorScore seal on laminate flooring or check its VOC emissions against emissions standards for, say, engineered wood. It starts at about $2.50 per square foot.

Clockwise from opposite bottom: Green flooring options include concrete with recycled fly ash content, recycled stone, and sustainably harvested woods.

adobe

DESCRIPTION A durable mixture often consisting of clay, sand and straw. Installed in three layers: a thick, tamped-down base; a thin, troweled-on layer; and a brushed-on topcoat. Sealed with natural oils and beeswax. Colors range from concrete grays to brick reds to barrel browns; custom tints available.

PROS Retains heat very well. Insulates and does not fade in sunlight. Offers a truly seamless look and can tightly abut—or even continue up—walls and stairs. Can be laid over existing subflooring. Typically sourced locally, therefore little fuel expenditure.

CONS Installation is expensive and labor-intensive. Not do-it-yourself friendly, yet few adobe specialists available. Can take up to a month to install and dry. Cannot be laid over an existing slab. Susceptible to cracking. Standing water can cause surface oils to blister; can erode when exposed to continuous moisture. Not good for extremely wet or humid climates, for heavy-traffic areas, or for kitchens and bathrooms. Time-consuming to repair.

MAINTENANCE Keep dry and sweep weekly, damp-mop monthly, and oil and wax annually. Scratches and cracks can be sanded or patched with wet adobe, then reoiled, rewaxed and buffed.

PRICE RANGE $15 to $20 per square foot (installed).

certified wood

DESCRIPTION Wood harvested in a way that preserves biodiversity and natural habitats, and meets the standards set by the Forest Stewardship Council, a third-party watchdog group. Wide range of colors, patterns and species available.

PROS Long-lasting. Available in unfinished and prefinished forms, and in nail-down, glue-down and floating versions. Can be laid over existing flooring. Most repairs easy to do.

CONS Difficult to install and refinish yourself if using solid hardwood. Costs more than conventional lumber. Can expand or contract in extremely humid or arid conditions. Can fade in sunlight. Limited stock and poor distribution systems can mean a three- to six-week wait time. Like uncertified wood, some species contain resins that can cause contact dermatitis and respiratory distress. Importing exotics results in significant fuel expenditures.

MAINTENANCE Keep dry. Sweep with a fine-bristle broom or vacuum with a soft brush attachment weekly; damp-mop regularly. Refinish at first sign of wear. Repair cracks and gouges with wood filler, then stain and seal.

PRICE RANGE $4 (softwoods like pine) to $8 (exotics like teak) to $12 (premium grade hardwood) per square foot.

cork

DESCRIPTION Slabs or tiles made from the ground-up bark of cork oak trees. Hues and patterns vary, from uniform beige to woodsy walnut swirls to deep red. Can be custom-colored.

PROS Extremely durable. Helps insulate, maintain room temperature, cushion steps and dampen sound. Water-resistant; retains shape in humid, dry, hot and cold climates. Will return to form if compressed. Available in unfinished and prefinished versions, and in glue-down and floating types. Can be laid over existing flooring; appearance close to seamless. Easy to install and repair.

CONS Can be torn by sharp objects, so not ideal for homes with pets. Can be bleached by sunlight. Not suited to very wet areas like bathrooms or kitchens, or anywhere there is standing water. Demand beginning to outstrip supply, boosting costs and wait times. Imported from the western Mediterranean, resulting in large expenditures of fuel.

MAINTENANCE Keep dry and vacuum weekly; wipe down with an antistatic cloth to discourage dirt and dust. Reseal wax floors and recoat polyurethaned floors once a year.

PRICE RANGE $5 to $8 per square foot.

linoleum

DESCRIPTION Biodegradable mixture of powdered cork, wood flour, ground limestone, linseed oil, pine rosin and pigments typically affixed to a jute backing. Wide variety of colors, patterns and textures, from solid primaries and pastels to wood grains to mock crocodile skins.

PROS Easily available. Long-lasting and retains shape in damp, dry, hot, humid or cold conditions. Resistant to fading; near seamless appearance. Ideal for bathrooms and kitchens. Can be laid over existing flooring. Cushions steps. Strengthens over time. Available in glue-down and floating versions. Tile form is easy to install and repair.

CONS May show drag marks, abrasions and scratches, so not suited for homes with pets. Hot water can discolor surface. Sheet versions can be difficult to install and repair. Often shipped from Europe, which requires significant fuel expenditures.

MAINTENANCE Sweep or vacuum frequently and damp-mop as necessary. Remove marks with a nylon kitchen pad; use a scouring brush on stubborn stains, then reseal. Recoat as needed.

PRICE RANGE $5 to $9 per square foot.

bamboo

DESCRIPTION Made from a quick-growing grass that is as tough as wood. Mature shoots are cut down and sliced into strips, then glued together horizontally (revealing the grain) or vertically (showing even stripes). Colors range from bleached blonds to reds and browns.

PROS Durable, with a uniform, woodlike texture. Available in unfinished and prefinished forms, and in nail-down, glue-down and floating versions (the latter can be laid over existing flooring without using hardware or adhesives). Simple to moderately difficult to install.

CONS Like wood, may swell in extremely humid or wet environments and shrink in very dry environments; not ideal for kitchens or bathrooms. Fades in sunlight. Darker-colored products more susceptible to scratching. Sourced primarily in the Far East, so much fuel is consumed during importation.

MAINTENANCE Keep dry (wipe up spills with a damp cloth, then a dry one). Sweep with a fine-bristled broom or vacuum with a soft brush attachment weekly, and damp-mop monthly. Reseal at first sign of wear.

PRICE RANGE $5 to $8 per square foot.

LINOLEUM

In use since the mid-1800s, linoleum has many environmental benefits that are fueling its big comeback. The natural raw materials used to create linoleum—linseed oil, pine resin, wood flour, cork flour, ecologically responsible pigments and jute—are available in abundance. Furthermore, the plants and trees that supply linoleum's raw materials also contribute to the production of oxygen and the reduction of carbon dioxide in the atmosphere, helping to contain greenhouse gases in the atmosphere. Its raw materials require little energy to harvest and it can be recycled or safely disposed of in landfills, as it is fully biodegradable. It does not release harmful substances or gases and its patterns are dyed all the way through to the backing, ensuring even wear. For installation, use adhesives that are solvent-free and meet all low-VOC requirements. Make sure to purchase natural linoleum. Some experts have raised concerns about aldehydes that outgas from the linseed oil used to make linoleum. Although linoleum's faint smell may not appeal to some, linseed oil is a natural antimicrobial agent, making linoleum a good choice for kitchens. It is not recommended for areas where moisture may seep through the subfloor, such as concrete in basements. Dry cleaning methods are preferred to wet cleaning, so linoleum flooring reduces wastewater. It lasts about 30 to 40 years, and generally costs about $4 per square foot.

RUBBER

Generally used for play or outdoor areas where nonslip surfaces are needed, natural virgin rubber flooring is manufactured from latex, the sap of rubber trees, which typically grow in tropical areas, mostly in Asia. But rubber can also be produced synthetically. Some rubber flooring is made from recycled materials, such as rubber tires, which are abundant in North America. Converting these materials into rubber flooring requires a fair amount of energy, but transport costs are generally lower than for imports, so recycled rubber flooring is generally less expensive and more durable than virgin rubber flooring.

Rubber is chemically stable, although it does outgas slightly, giving it a distinctive smell, but emission of toxic elements is low. Because of its natural tackiness, it can be installed without adhesives, lessening its outgassing potential compared with other materials. It is also easy to clean and

A rug made of natural fibers provides softness and texture atop a certified sustainably harvested wood floor in a room by architect Rick Renner.

durable, lasting about 20 years. Rubber flooring usually is flammable, however, and can be problematic for people with allergies. You can purchase hypoallergenic products, but if you have sensitivities, use it only outdoors. It costs about $5 to $7 per square foot.

CARPETS AND RUGS

Since carpets and rugs are made from so many types of materials, some natural and some synthetic, their green properties must be evaluated first by their material type. Carpets and rugs made from any kind of natural material—

kinds require either an adhesive or carpet tacks. Because of outgassing concerns, ask your installer to unroll and air out the carpet in a well-ventilated area before installation, and to use only low-emitting adhesives. Ventilate the installation area, to the extent that you can, for 48 to 72 hours after installation.

According to the Carpet and Rug Institute, the carpet industry is making efforts to minimizing carpet's impact on the environment by emphasizing what it calls the "3 Rs," which stand for reduce, reuse and recycle. When carpet reaches the end of its life, it is reused to make new carpet or is recycled into a variety of products. The Green Label and Green Label Plus programs from the Carpet and Rug Institute also provide customers with a means by which to know whether they are purchasing the lowest-emitting carpet, adhesive and cushion products on the market. To achieve the Carpet and Rug Institute's Green Label Plus certification, a carpet must meet California's most rigorous Section 01350 standard, which tests

from wool, cotton and silk to coir, sisal and jute—are eco-friendly in that they don't outgas, unless they've been finished or dyed with toxic substances or have synthetic backings. Natural fibers have different levels of durability, however, and some, such as sisal and jute, are prone to mildew and should not be used in humid locations. If you choose a natural-fiber rug or carpet, place it over a natural carpet pad, such as one made of 100 percent cotton, wool, jute, horsehair or felt.

Most carpet, however, is made from petroleum-based materials, such as nylon or polyester. Commonly criticized for its outgassing of VOCs in the home, synthetic carpeting is sometimes made from post-consumer plastic soft-drink containers, and recycled carpet padding can be made from old carpet padding or reclaimed carpet fibers. But just 4 percent of carpet is recycled—though the Carpet and Rug Institute (CRI) says this figure will increase to 20 to 25 percent by 2012—and about 30 percent of all foam cushion used for carpet padding in the United States comes from imported waste fibers. Binders used to make synthetic carpets and padding may outgas for years after installation, with varying levels of emissions and toxicity. And wall-to-wall carpets of all

Atop refinished solid wood floors, a sunny wool rug adds shots of color and pattern to a sparely furnished room by the Otto Baat Group.

Resources

These websites offer ample information on various indoor building materials, including certification standards information, analysis and recycling ideas.

- greenhomeguide.com A web-based resource featuring eco-friendly floor refinishing ideas and other green tips, case studies, expert Q&A articles, and directories of products and services
- wfca.org The World Floor Covering Association
- carpet-rug.org The Carpet and Rug Institute
- healthybuilding.net The Healthy Building Network
- vinylinfo.org The Vinyl Institute
- fsc.org The Forest Stewardship Council
- greenseal.org An independent, science-based, nonprofit third-party certifier of green products
- greenguard.org The Greenguard Environmental Institute
- healthhouse.org American Lung Association Health House
- rfci.com The Resilient Floor Covering Institute
- greenerchoices.org A website offering information and ideas on recycling and pollution
- scscertified.com Scientific Certifications Systems
- www.pca.state.mn.us/oea/carpet/index.cfm For information on the national agreement on recycling carpet

for emissions of individual VOCs rather than just the overall level of VOCs. Although the carpet label may list the material as wool, nylon or some other synthetic fiber, it's the unlisted substances, such as chemical additives for controlling mildew, fungus and rot, or elements in the primary and secondary backings, that are most responsible for outgassing.

Once installed, carpeting has excellent sound- and thermal-insulating properties. But it's practically impossible to keep it truly clean. Furthermore, synthetic carpet never breaks down and is one of the big contributors to greenhouse gas emissions in our landfills. While carpet is the softest flooring material considered here, it is one of the least durable, and may require replacement about every 11 years. It costs from about $4 and up per square foot.

VINYL

Some flooring types are simply at odds with the environment, and polyvinyl chloride (PVC) flooring is one of them. Because it's relatively inexpensive and easy to install, it's one of the most popular flooring choices—14 billion pounds of it are produced each year in North America. But it presents a health hazard across its entire life cycle, from production and installation to use and disposal. Its manufacturing creates poisons, including vinyl chloride, ethylene dichloride and dioxin. It is a nonrenewable petroleum-based plastic, and the oil needed to make it often travels thousands of miles to get to North America, making it energy-inefficient to produce. Once it's installed, vinyl may outgas potentially harmful compounds for years. And when its useful life ends, it will not decay in landfills. Millions of pounds of vinyl tile are disposed of in landfills in the United States each year. However, the Vinyl Institute has claimed it is making progress in recycling the material. Available in sheets or tiles, it starts at about $2.50 per square foot.

Factors Affecting the Environmental Impact of Flooring Materials

Raw Materials Ideally, flooring materials should originate with a renewable substance, such as bamboo, wood, cork or plants. Ceramic tile and stone are plentiful but not renewable. Also consider products salvaged from existing structures or recycled materials.

Manufacture The less a material is modified during manufacture, the better. Stone, wood and bamboo require the least modification; cork, ceramic tile, linoleum, rubber flooring, and carpets and rugs require more energy to manufacture.

Transport Some flooring materials must be shipped great distances, increasing their embodied energy cost and total environmental impact. Try to choose materials that originate within 500 miles of your home to help keep embodied energy costs low.

Installation It may require cutting, sanding, sealing and adhesive application to attach a flooring material to the substrate in your house, which may in turn affect indoor air quality. If possible, opt for water-based adhesives rather than solvent-based options. Green Seal's adhesives standard sets 150 grams of VOCs per liter of product as a safe maximum.

Use and Maintenance After installation, most flooring will outgas various compounds—some inert, some potentially harmful—over long periods of time. To determine whether a flooring product is safe for the long term, look for the FloorScore seal, which was developed by Scientific Certification Systems, an environmental testing organization, in conjunction with the Resilient Floor Covering Institute, and certifies products as meeting California's tough Section 01350 requirements for indoor emissions. Maintenance and durability are also key issues. Less durable floors must be replaced more often, and high-maintenance floors can consume excess energy and expose you to harmful chemicals.

End of Life Consider what happens to your flooring after it's lived its useful life. Synthetic materials don't decay, but increasing amounts of them are now recycled. Stone can be crushed and reused as aggregate in tile or other applications. Linoleum, cork and wood are biodegradable or can be burned for energy.

Eco-Friendly Furniture and Accents

If you've put forth the effort to carefully craft an eco-friendly nest, then the last thing you'd want to do is feather it with furnishings and accents that can be harmful or unhealthy to you—or to the planet. Unfortunately, quite a bit of furniture is like a lot of standard houses—made with toxic materials and finishes, and fabricated and transported in wasteful, inefficient ways that pollute the environment. But like a growing number of building product manufacturers, many makers of home furnishings products—from bookshelves, tables and upholstered chairs to fabrics, mattresses and decorative pillows—are beginning to respond to the call for sustainable designs. And interested organizations are doing their part to create industry-specific standards for evaluating the environmental impact of home furnishings products and manufacturing processes, making it easier for consumers to understand just how green their home goods choices really are.

Many of the same environmental issues related to building products and interior surface materials apply to home furnishings, too. For example, a lot of wood furnishings are treated with stains or finishes or made with adhesives that outgas VOCs and pollute indoor air, and the disposal of these hazardous chemicals contaminates the environment. Upholstered furnishings, on the other hand, are often made with synthetic fabrics and foams that sit in landfills after they've outlived their usefulness. Even drapery and upholstery textiles made of natural materials, such as cotton, can be problematic. These fabrics are usually made with fibers harvested from crops grown in soil that's been coated with polluting pesticides, and they are also often treated with stain-repellants or other finishes that can cause problems for people with chemical sensitivities. Furthermore, the energy required to harvest, mine, manufacture or transport home furnishings is often produced using nonrenewable resources, which in turn release harmful emissions into the ozone.

WHAT IS SUSTAINABLE DESIGN?

As with exterior and interior building materials, choosing green furnishings, fabrics and accents invariably means making trade-offs among performance, quality, beauty, durability and price. Yet, as awareness of energy and environmental issues continues to grow, most responsible home furnishings manufacturers are now striving to create products, refine manufacturing processes and develop business practices in ways that are as eco-friendly as possible. And their efforts are often yielding unanticipated benefits. Not only are these companies reducing their carbon footprints, they're often reducing costs and making their businesses and their communities more sustainable, too.

To help clarify and define just what sustainable design is for furnishings manufacturers, retailers and consumers alike, two organizations have recently developed guidelines and certification programs specifically for the furniture industry. The Sustainable Furnishings Council, a nonprofit industry association founded in 2006, requires that its members minimize carbon emissions, waste-stream pollutants, unrecyclable content and primary materials from unsustainable sources for any product platform under its control. Its more than 250 members, which include manufacturers, retailers, environmental organizations and individuals, use its "life cycle assessment" approach to analyze the environmental impact of their products and establish what is known as a verifiable "chain of custody," which tracks the flow of wood products from their source to their final user and end-product. Known for its rigorous compliance with established sustainability standards, the organization launched a public advertising and in-store tagging program in 2008, which enables consumers to identify retailers and products that meet or exceed its sustainability standards.

The other organization that has defined industry-specific environmental guidelines for furniture is the American Home Furnishings Alliance. Launched in 1999, its voluntary Enhancing Furniture's Environmental Culture (EFEC) system supports registered companies in analyzing the environmental impact of their processes, raw materials and finished products

Previous page: Old chairs get new life with fresh upholstery and slipcovers. Opposite: A pair of Marcel Breuer Wassily chairs brings timeless style to a room by architect Rick Renner. Above: Old furnishings mixing with new brings eco-friendly sophistication to a room by designer Janie Hirsch.

To encourage and acknowledge sustainable design and business practices in the home furnishings industry even more, the AHFA, in conjunction with Cargill BiOH polyols, launched the Sage Awards program in 2008. The program seeks to discover and recognize industry innovators in the realm of green design and business practices, and finalists in the inaugural competition included Cisco Brothers, a California-based furniture company, the Hickory Chair Company, a North Carolina–based furniture company, and Valley Forge, a Florida-based textile manufacturer. The winner, the Hickory Chair Company, announced at the AHFA's Sustainability Summit in Greensboro, North Carolina, in 2008, was honored for its company-wide commitment to environmental stewardship. The effort resulted in the implementation of more than 1,200 improvements—from reducing energy consumption to eliminating non-value-added operations, improving productivity and reducing material

on a facility-by-facility basis. To complement this effort, the Alliance unveiled its more comprehensive Sustainable by Design certification program in 2007. Sustainable by Design requires companies first to complete EFEC registration for all their domestic facilities, then to implement sustainable business practices throughout their entire supply chain. At this book's presstime, companies with facilities that have passed the EFEC audit include Stanley, La-Z-Boy, Vaughan, Bernhardt, C.R. Laine, Hickory Chair, Lea Industries, American Drew, Kincaid and Vaughan-Bassett.

Resources

For more information on green furnishings and accents or the materials used to make them, visit these websites:

- sustainablefurniturecouncil.org For information on members of the Sustainable Furnishings Council
- sustainablebydesign.us For information on the American Home Furniture Alliance's Sustainable by Design program
- fscus.org For information on wood products certified by the Forest Stewardship Council
- greenguard.org For information on Greenguard-certified mattresses
- sfiprogram.org For information on wood products certified by Sustainable Forestry Initiative
- imo.ch/index.php?seite=imo_services_textile_en For information on organic cotton fabric certified by the Institute of Marketecology
- treefarmsystem.org For information on the American Tree Farm System by the Programme for the Endorsement of Forest Certification schemes (PEFC)
- ewg.org For the Environmental Working Group's list of PBDE-free products (flame retardants)
- aafa.org For information on products certified by the Asthma and Allergy Foundation of America

usage. These measures enabled the company to reduced its landfill waste by hundreds of tons in 2007 and save $450,000 in fuel oil expenses last year, while growing its profitability. In the past three years its workforce has grown by about 30 employees per year, prices have held for over five years, and its employees still receive raises and bonuses.

In addition to these organizations, some of the reliable certifiers of building products, such as Greenguard, the Forest Stewardship Council, and the Sustainable Forestry Initiative, can also be resources for more information on green furnishings. Greenguard, for example, has certified home furnishings products ranging from window treatments and office furniture to case goods, seating and tables.

Since sustainable design, manufacturing and business practices may be evaluated on many levels and are virtually impossible to quantify simply, an overview of some of the environmental issues affecting various categories of furnishings and the green strategies employed by a few companies who lead the green movement will establish some context. Wood furnishings and case goods vary dramatically in terms of quality, composition and construction—and their eco-friendly characteristics are diverse, too. By understanding the materials used to make these furnishings, consumers can better compare their sustainable attributes.

Opposite: Made with an FSC-certified frame and organic cotton batting, this lounge chair from Pure Furniture is glamorous and eco-friendly.

Above: Vintage furniture and accents, cotton fabrics and a flat-weave rug give this beach house room relaxed, low-maintenance appeal.

WOOD FURNISHINGS AND CASE GOODS

Wood and Construction

Wood furnishings range from affordable machine-made ready-to-assemble (RTA) pieces to costly handmade pieces crafted with age-old woodworking techniques. Lower- and mid-priced wood furniture is made of a wood veneer or a paper laminate attached to a core of particleboard or plywood. Higher-end pieces are made of solid wood. The woods used to make the furniture may come from domestic forests of rapidly growing or abundant species, such as pine, basswood, beech wood or maple, or slow-growing or rare trees, such as chestnut,

mahogany or oak. They may also come from exotic forests in such places as Asia, Africa or Brazil, and might include species such as teak or zebrawood. Some furnishings made from bamboo and rattan can be combined with and look like wood, but bamboo is actually a grass and rattan is a vine.

The greenest options for wood furnishings are those made from solid, abundant woods grown and harvested from certified sustainably managed domestic forests, as the energy expended in transporting the woods to the manufacturing facility will be low. However, for those who prefer the look of furnishings made from exotic woods, choosing pieces that

have been certified by the FSC or other reputable third-party organizations will assure you that the woods from which they are made were grown and harvested sustainably. Like kitchen cabinets constructed in a similar manner, wood furnishings made with veneers or paper laminates affixed to compressed wood or plywood substrates outgas various levels of VOCs. Furnishings that meet emissions standards established by Greenguard or the California Air Resources Board (CARB) assure minimal emissions levels.

FINISHES AND ADHESIVES

Like kitchen cabinets, wood furnishings are usually treated with stains, paints or finishes and may be made with adhesives that also outgas VOCs. While many people who love fine furniture appreciate the depth and richness of oil-based finishes, those with chemical sensitivities can suffer from the VOC emissions of these solvent-based sealers. In response to the demand for healthier furnishings, many wood furniture manufacturers are now offering more products coated with water- or soy-based, low-VOC, low-HAP (hazardous air pollutant) coatings or low-emitting UF (urea formaldehyde) resins. Others rely on environmentally friendly and health-conscious oils and waxes.

A FEW GOOD GREEN SOURCES

Gat Creek and Caperton, two manufacturers of high-value solid wood furnishings and founding members of the Sustainable Furnishings Council, have always embraced sustainable design principals in their manufacturing processes and products. Among the many green practices employed by these companies in the donation of sawdust generated in their facilities to local farmers as animal bedding. Selamat, a manufacturer of award-winning indoor/outdoor furnishings, creates its furnishings from durable teak, rattan and bamboo harvested from government-certified green forests in Asia. Sauder, a manufacturer of RTA furniture, uses 95 percent recycled postindustrial material in its laminated wood-product furnishings, which are also CARB-certified and shipped via flat-pack methods that reduce its transportation carbon footprint. IKEA, another manufacturer and retailer of solid and veneered wood furnishings, sources its products from sustainably managed forests and meets the European E1 emissions standards. The greenest options for wood furnishings,

Opposite: New and old wood pieces and upholstered furnishings covered in natural fabrics bring sustainable style to a room by Janie Hirsch.

Above: Salvaged flea market furniture and collectibles offer an affordable way to bring eco-friendly flavor to a room.

Reducing Exposure to Formaldehyde in the Home

Formaldehyde is used to add permanent-press qualities to bedding and draperies, and in adhesives and preservatives in some furniture paints and coating products. In homes, the most significant sources of formaldehyde are likely to be pressed-wood products made with adhesives that contain urea-formaldehyde (UF) resins. Pressed-wood products used in furnishings include particleboard, used as shelving and in cabinetry and furniture; hardwood plywood paneling, used in cabinets and furniture; and medium-density fiberboard, for drawer fronts and furniture tops. Medium-density fiberboard contains a higher resin-to-wood ratio than any other UF pressed-wood product and is generally recognized as being the highest formaldehyde-emitting pressed wood product.

Ask about the formaldehyde content of pressed-wood furniture products before you purchase them. If you've experienced adverse reactions to formaldehyde, try to avoid the use of pressed-wood products and other formaldehyde-emitting goods altogether. But even if you haven't experienced such reactions, you can reduce your exposure as much as possible by purchasing exterior-grade products, which emit less formaldehyde. For more information on formaldehyde and consumer products, call the EPA Toxic Substance Control Act (TSCA) assistance line (202-554-1404).

however, are those made from reclaimed lumber acquired from existing structures that have been deemed irreparable. The Old Wood Co., based in Asheville, North Carolina, offers stunning consoles and cocktail and accent tables that are made from reclaimed woods and finished with soy-based and other nontoxic finishes.

Furniture Shopping Tip

According to the AHFA, approximately six out of every 10 consumers wish they could repurchase a piece of furniture simply because they feel they didn't buy it right the first time around. Recent research commissioned by the American Furniture Manufacturers Association also found that more than half of those surveyed would be willing to pay more for home furnishings if they had reliable information to help them identify construction. For the AHFA's consumer's guide to smart shopping, visit *ahfanews.com*.

Opposite top and bottom, and above: A beautiful weathered hutch, an elegant tiered side table and a stunning curio cabinet from the Hickory Chair Company are manufactured domestically, and made with high-quality materials and finishes and classic styling.

Left top: A lovely side table from the Old Wood Co. was crafted from reclaimed wood and coated with a nontoxic, soy-based finish.
Left bottom: A pretty, solid-wood painted Loire side table from Caperton was sustainably designed and manufactured in the U.S.

UPHOLSTERED FURNITURE, TEXTILES AND SOFT FURNISHINGS

Many manufacturers of upholstered furniture today offer at least one line of eco-friendly furniture, and some offer certain green characteristics as standard features in all of their furniture lines.

Frames and Springs

The same environmental issues that affect wood furnishings and case goods apply to upholstered furnishings made with wood frames. In a move toward increased sustainability, several upholstered chair and sofa manufacturers are now creating frames made from certified sustainable woods and finishing them with low-VOC, low-HAP coatings. They're also using water-based glues and crafting the frames using environmentally friendly manufacturing processes. Some manufacturers are also using recycled iron ore or metal to create the springs that support the seat cushions of upholstered pieces.

Cushions and Padding

Most upholstered furniture is covered with padding and topped with cushions made from synthetic foam or latex. Since synthetic foams, particularly polyurethane foams, break down and emit particles of harmful chemical dust into the atmosphere over time, more manufacturers are beginning to offer a variety of eco-friendly alternatives to pad and cushion their upholstered pieces. Some of these options include filler made from recycled plastic bottles, and foams made from bio-, soy- or other plant-based, renewable materials. Others offer stuffing made from natural materials, such as wool, kapok, down or cotton batting. While these natural materials are more environmentally friendly than petroleum-based foams, some—such as down, kapok and latex—can be allergens for people with sensitivities. The most eco-friendly foams and padding materials should be free of polybrominated diphenyl ethers (PBDEs), a family of flame retardants that were once added to furniture, car upholstery and mattresses, but have since been voluntarily taken off the market by manufacturers after concerns were raised about their toxicity.

Fabrics and Finishes

Whether they are used as furniture upholstery or to make other soft furnishings, such as draperies, shades and cushion covers, fabrics made of natural fibers—like cotton, linen, hemp and silk—are growing in popularity for the home. Yet synthetic fabrics offer benefits of colorfastness and durability, making them preferred choices in certain circumstances, such as in outdoor settings or family rooms. And when these fabrics are made with recycled content, they can be regarded as environmentally friendly, too.

Nevertheless, all decorative fabrics, even if they are made of natural fibers, are difficult to evaluate from a green perspective, partly because of a shortage of sustainable standards or certifications programs against which to judge them. For example, just because a fabric is labeled 100 percent natural doesn't mean it's 100 percent organic. One way for a cotton fabric to be certified as 100 percent organic is to pass the certification standards established by the IMO, a Swiss-based international agency that inspects, certifies and assures the quality of various eco-friendly products. The organization is accredited by the Swiss Accreditation Service (SAS), according to the international standard for certification, and is also accredited by the USDA, according to the American National Organic Program's standard for certification. Before the IMO will certify a cotton fabric as organic, the soil supporting the cotton plants that yielded its fibers must be verified to have been pesticide-free for three years, and no pesticides or synthetic fertilizers can have been used in their cultivation.

The most eco-friendly fabrics are either left in their natural unbleached, undyed state, or colored or printed with IMO-certified, low-impact, earth-friendly dyes, which contain fewer metal compounds than standard dyes. Most home decor fabrics are also finished with a sizing or with stain protection treatments that may contain perfluorinated or other chemicals, which should be avoided by those with chemical sensitivities.

Opposite: Earth-friendly furniture from Lee Industries' Naturall EE line feature certified wood frames, soy-foam cushions and natural fabrics.

Right: Set amid antiques, new sofas and chairs are covered in natural fiber fabrics in a room by Elaine Griffin for the Twin Maples show house.

Good Green Resources

Several manufacturers of upholstered seating are producing eco-friendly options. Cisco Brothers, an industry leader in sustainable and eco-friendly furniture, makes its pieces using the highest quality natural materials, such as soy-based foam, nontoxic glues and FSC-certified woods. The Hickory Chair Company, a 97-year-old manufacturer of fine furniture, has developed an Environmental Stewardship Policy, which has enabled the company to reduce its carbon footprint by using wood dust from its factories to fuel its boiler, reduce its costs, grow its business and help sustain the local community through increased employment. Its furnishings are also made from domestic wood purchased from sustainable sources, and many of its fabrics are made of natural or organic fibers. As of the end of 2008, C.R. Laine was the first furniture company to complete the requirements of the EFEC system and achieve Sustainable by Design certification, and its qualified furnishings are the first to bear a Sustainable by Design tag. Rowe Furniture, a founding member of the Sustainable Furnishings Council, recently launched its eco-friendly EcoRowe initiative, which includes eco-friendly manufacturing processes, eco-cushion cores, natural fiber fabrics, and several certified organic cotton fabrics finished with an eco-wash process that uses biodegradable solvents to prevent color migration. And Lee Industries' earth-friendly NaturalLee furniture includes FSC- and SFI-certified wood frames, soy-based cushions, and water-based finishes.

Healthy Bouquets

Did you know that your fresh flower habit may be hazardous to your health? Conventionally grown blossoms are coated with chemical fertilizers and pesticides that contaminate soil and groundwater.

As a healthier option, choose flowers that are either certified organic by VeriFlora (a sustainability guarantee) or biodynamic (a growing method with even stricter standards). Both are pesticide-free. These blooms aren't easy to find, but you can purchase them at many Whole Foods locations. You can also browse and special-order from the extensive online floral offerings from Organic Bouquet by visiting *organicbouquet.com*.

Right: Cotton fabric in a lively nature-inspired pattern lends an additional earth-friendly touch to an upholstered piece from Lee Industries' NaturalLee line.
Center left and right: The Bo side chair from Cisco Brothers is made of sustainable materials, and an ottoman from C.R. Laine is among the first furnishings to earn the AHFA's Sustainable by Design certification.

Opposite left: Slipcovered in a solid natural fiber fabric, a traditional chair gets a clean, environmentally friendly update.
Opposite right: A stunning settee from Pure Furniture is green and glamorous.
Above left, and bottom: A contemporary wing chair and classic modern sofa from Rowe Furniture's EcoRowe line feature eco-friendly cushions and natural fiber fabrics.

MATTRESSES AND BEDDING

The quality of your mattress will profoundly impact the quality of your sleep. But given the number of synthetic materials and chemicals used in the manufacture of most mattresses, it can also have a profound effect on your health. With so many different manufacturers and mattress products in the marketplace, weighing the options in comfort, cost and durability is difficult enough. But from a green perspective, it is also important to assess the chemicals that mattresses may emit and the effects they may have on our health.

Mattress manufacturers often appeal to consumers with promises of the best sleeping comfort, without mentioning the impact that a mattress's materials may have on the air they breathe. Yet many commercial mattresses are manufactured using polyurethane foam, synthetic fabrics, chemical fire retardants, toxic dyes, formaldehyde, antifungicides, pesticide-treated cotton and stain-resistant chemicals, and the potentially toxic VOCs outgassed from these elements can cause allergic reactions and other health problems.

In response to consumers' concern about the harmful effects these chemicals may impose, many manufacturers have begun to produce healthier or organic mattresses. These mattresses are often made with a combination of certified organic cotton, natural rubber, and wool, and do not include metal springs, which are conductive of electricity that can disturb our equilibrium. (Because metal attracts electromagnetic fields that can interfere with our bodies' natural electrical systems, it's best to choose wood bed frames in lieu of metal ones, too.) This combination of materials can be made in various thicknesses and firmnesses, and will provide good, chemical-free support.

Untreated wool is naturally fire-resistant, repels mites, mold and mildew, and wicks away moisture, but for the small number of people who are severely allergic to wool, a pure latex mattress may provide a healthier alternative. Natural latex provides a comfortable surface that molds to a body's

contours and can last up to 20 years without sagging. But for people with sensitivities to latex, testing any mattress containing this material before buying it is advisable, since most mattresses are not returnable after purchase. While cotton is a comfortable, breathable natural-fiber fabric, the cotton crops from which it is made are often cultivated with toxic pesticides. If possible, choose a mattress containing only certified organic cotton batting.

To verify a manufacturer's green claims about a mattress, consumers should find out whether the product is certified by an authorized program or organization. In 2006, Greenguard certified the first bedding products for low chemical emissions.

Opposite: An antique screen was repurposed as a headboard for a bed topped with crisp cotton bedding in a room designed by Janie Hirsch.

Above: Stunning eco-friendly silk fabrics and bedding from Lulan enrich an antique four-poster bed in the home of designer Eve Blossom.

Bedding and Pillows

Bedding and pillows made of natural materials, such as cotton, silk, linen, wool or cotton flannel, are the best green options. But even natural bedding elements can pose certain health hazards. Unless they're made of certified-organic natural cotton, all-cotton sheets may contain pesticide residue and emit VOCs from synthetic dyes and permanent-press finishes. Wool blankets, on the other hand, may be treated with moth-proof finishes. The greenest bedding is made of undyed, certified-organic fabrics.

If asthma or allergies are a concern, make sure to buy a pillow that minimizes these issues and is certified by a credible association, such as the Asthma and Allergy Foundation of America, which, before certifying their products, puts them through a stringent scientific testing process.

In many ways the bedroom is the most important room in the house. It's the place where we rest and regenerate—and spend one third of our lives. As we sleep, our bodies shed metabolic waste and restore our natural electrical systems and internal organs. So our beds and bedding should be the first green furnishings choices we make for our home.

Green DIY Pillow Recipe

This green pillow recipe, adapted from PointClickHome.com, comes from Q Collection, a textile manufacturer that chooses every ingredient for its pillows with the planet's health in mind.

INGREDIENTS

1.5 yard of Climatex Lifeguard FR Natural Satin Wool (60 percent wool, 40 percent viscose)

Needle and cotton thread

4 yards natural cotton piping

Pins

Sewing machine

20" metal zipper, recycled content

22" free-range down and feather insert

DIRECTIONS

Cut the satin wool fabric into two 23" squares. Baste the organic cotton piping around one piece of fabric. Lay one square on top of the other, right sides facing, and baste one side with ½" seam allowance. Press open the seam, pin the zipper facedown over the seam and stitch in place. Sew the two squares together with cotton thread, leaving ½" seam allowance. Open the seam over the zipper. Turn right side out and insert pillow form.

ECO-FRIENDLY DETAILS

- The 100 percent natural textiles are made of wool and beech viscose, both renewable resources.
- The insert's free-range down and feathers are humanely plucked from free-range birds raised without hormones.
- The low-impact dye contains no toxic substances.
- The organic cotton is grown without use of pesticides.

CLEANUP TIP

Take the leftover Climatex fabric, which is biodegradable, and add it to your compost pile. It makes great mulch.

Above left: A hand-knit wool coverlet brings a cozy, personal touch of earth-friendly warmth to a contemporary bedroom.

Opposite: Turning fabric remnants, magazine photos and fallen leaves into art is an eco-wise way to add color and personality to a room.

Green and Clean

CLEANING PRODUCTS

Previous page: A mix of durable, easy-to-clean tiles add color and texture to an eco-conscious bath. Above: Ample storage above and below the counter keeps a vanity area looking neat and clean. Opposite: Sliding glass doors allow for easy natural ventilation.

Once you've cultivated a good green home by choosing energy-efficient appliances and healthy, sustainable materials and furnishings, the last thing you'd want to do is undermine your good intentions with cleaning supplies that introduce more toxic substances than they remove. Unfortunately, all too often that is just what happens when we clean. Even when you look at a cleaning product's label, it's virtually impossible to know whether it is biodegradable or contains harmful chemicals without knowledge of its ingredients and their chemistry. The fact that manufacturers are not required by law to list all of their ingredients—unless they are active disinfectants or known to be potentially hazardous—makes it even more challenging to understand the true level of toxicity in any given household cleaner. And regulatory agencies are often slow in identifying which of the vast number of products in the marketplace are unsafe.

But choosing the least-toxic products is the best strategy to keeping a healthy home. Doing so will reduce the risk of harm not only to you and your family in the home but also to the planet when the products are disposed of. Fortunately, new suppliers of eco-friendly cleaning supplies have begun to emerge, making it easier to safely clean your home. Mainstream makers of cleaning supplies, such as Procter & Gamble and Clorox, are now producing more eco-friendly products, too.

While green household cleaners can cost more than their conventional counterparts, the health-preserving—and often aromatic—perks are worth the extra money. Yet, some of the more mainstream options, such as Clorox's Green Works line, which is made from 99 percent natural ingredients, can cost just pennies more than their toxic counterparts—and they're available everywhere.

To be sure a cleaning product is truly green, choose one from a manufacturer that voluntarily opts to fully disclose all of its ingredients, as some environmentally responsible companies such as Ecover, Isabella Smith's Maison Belle, and Seventh Generation do. Another way to be sure of the eco-friendliness of a green cleaning product is to look for

the Green Seal label or the EcoLogo stamp of approval from TerraChoice, a company that certifies green products. Both labels certify that products have been independently verified as environmentally sound and meet the same strict standards.

Look at the Labels

If you simply must purchase a cleaning product containing harmful or toxic chemicals, then your main concern should be reducing exposure. Look for the various warnings listed on labels and understand what they mean so that you can take the necessary precautions to limit harm to your health and the environment.

All household cleaners that contain known hazardous chemicals are required to display a warning label that spells out potential risks, along with precautionary steps and first aid instructions. Toilet bowl, oven, and drain cleaners often bear labels listing the words "Poison" or "Danger." These products are corrosive, extremely flammable, highly toxic or poisonous, and are more harmful than those labeled "Warning" or "Caution," which can be used as catchall terms for various hazards. So for labels containing these terms, you'll need to look for phrases that identify specific adverse affects, such as "Causes burns" or "May be fatal if swallowed." Products with labels bearing the word "irritants" contain substances that cause injury or inflammation on contact, while those listing the word "corrosives" contain chemicals that destroy tissue. "Sensitizers" are ingredients that can cause allergic reactions and chronic adverse health effects that become evident only after repeated exposure.

Bear in mind that because there are few standard definitions or third-party organizations that verify claims listed on most cleaning supplies, certain terms, such as "nontoxic," "natural," "environmentally friendly" and "green" cannot necessarily be taken at face value. Only the term "biodegradable," which implies the product or its container safely breaks down in a reasonably short period of time, is loosely defined by the federal government. Arthur Weissman, president and CEO of Green Seal, a leading nonprofit green-cleaning certification organization, offers the following tips on what to look out for and what to avoid when choosing cleaning products.

Above: Nontoxic, biodegradable cleaning products from companies such as Maison Belle and Biokleen offer healthier alternatives to many commercial cleaners. Opposite: A small bath with limited surface area is easier to keep clean than a large one.

Seek

- **Citrus- or hydrogen peroxide–based sanitizers or disinfectants rather than chlorine-based ones** Chlorine can form organic compounds that are toxic even in low doses. The product label will list the active ingredient.

- **Cleaning products that can be diluted with cold water from the tap rather than with hot water** The energy required to heat water has significant environmental impacts in terms of the use of fossil fuels, air and water pollution, etc.

- **Product packaging that is minimal and recyclable** Unnecessary packaging wastes resources and consumes space in landfills. Avoid multilayer packaging. The recyclability of a package is often indicated on the bottom of a bottle with the "chasing arrows" symbol. Plastics labeled 1 (PET) or 2 (HDPE) are recyclable in many areas, whereas 3 (PVC) is not.

- **Biodegradable products** Such products decompose in the environment into minerals, carbon dioxide and water. Products that do not biodegrade linger in the environment and may be absorbed by other organisms or cause harm in their active form. Many manufacturers make the claim that their product is biodegradable, but the lack of such a claim does not necessarily mean that the product is not biodegradable.

Avoid

- **"Toxic" hazard warnings on label** If a product has such a warning, it can be very harmful to anyone who is exposed to it. By law, such a warning must appear on the product label.

- **Disinfectants for most home uses** In general, thorough cleaning will provide the necessary sanitation for most home situations. Cleaning areas for those with compromised immune systems or baby-changing areas may require a sanitizer, in which case a benign formula should be used according to the instructions. Labels will indicate whether the product is registered as a disinfectant or sanitizer.

- **Products containing potentially harmful but commonly used ingredients,** such as alkylphenol ethoxylates (APEs), certain glycol ethers, such as 2-butoxyethanol, or heavy metals, such as chromium or selenium. Although most household cleaners will not generally cause harm if used as recommended because of the low levels of exposure, the presence of potentially harmful ingredients may pose an unnecessary risk, especially to children or the elderly. Some common cleaning ingredients may be possible endocrine disrupters or possible carcinogens.

- **Products with any significant amount of phosphate (above 0.5%)** Phosphates cause problems in water bodies, contaminating water and stressing aquatic life.

- **Products with high levels of volatile organic compounds (VOCs)** Such products can contribute to indoor or outdoor air pollution and may cause respiratory distress or other illnesses indoors. The VOC level is unlikely to be indicated on product labels, so to find out about these substances you'll need to contact the manufacturer.

- **Products which contain a builder known as EDTA,** which stands for ethylenediaminetetraacetic acid. This substance is not biodegradable. Note that product labels may or may not specify the aforementioned toxic ingredients.

Natural Green Cleaners

One way to offset the potential extra cost of one or two pricey eco-friendly products is to make your own cleaners that cost next to nothing. Some of the greenest cleaning ingredients may already be sitting on your pantry shelf or in your medicine cabinet. Cream of tartar, for example, removes stains from sinks, tubs and aluminum pans, while baking soda can absorb odors and removes fruit juice stains. Using common household ingredients, you can make your own less toxic cleaners right at home by following simple, reliable recipes that are often available on the Internet. Remember, though, that cleaning solutions made with food products, such as lemon juice, can spoil, so proper storage is essential. Here is a list of familiar household ingredients and a description of their common cleaning applications:

- **Baking soda (bicarbonate of soda)** This mild alkali powder can be used to remove stains from tile, glass, oven doors and china. It can also be used to absorb odors, clean the inside of refrigerators or serve as a stain remover for fruit juices and other mild acids.

- **Borax** This powder or crystalline salt is a water softener and sanitizer. Sold in most grocery stores, it's an excellent all-around deodorizer and great freshener when added to laundry.

- **Castile soap** Once made from olive oil, but now possibly including other vegetable oils as well, this mild soap can be used for general-purpose cleaning. It is available in liquid or bar form.

- **Cream of tartar (potassium bitartrate)** This common baking ingredient is a mild acid that removes spots from aluminum cookware and can also be used as a sink and bathtub stain remover.

- **Hydrogen peroxide** Available in drugstores and supermarkets, this mild alternative to chlorine bleach can be used for stain removal, mild bleaching and killing germs.

- **Lemon juice** Not only does lemon juice lighten stains and cut grease, it also removes tarnish on brass, copper, bronze and aluminum (but not on silver).

- **White vinegar** Vinegar can be used to help kill germs and deodorize, remove some carpet stains, and clean coffeemakers, chrome, cookware and countertops. It can also be used to unclog drains. Note that while white vinegar has a slight scent while wet, when dry, it leaves no odor.

Simple Homemade Cleaning Solutions

For simple ways to put these ingredients to work in your kitchen or bath, try these recipes adapted from the Children's Health Environmental Coalition:

KITCHEN

- **Countertops** To make a simple soft scrub, mix a little baking soda and liquid soap until you get a consistency you like. Make only as much as you need, as it dries quickly.

- **Ovens** To make a healthy oven cleaner, mix 1 cup baking soda with ¼ cup washing soda, then add enough water to make a paste. Wearing rubber gloves (washing soda may irritate skin), apply the paste to greasy oven surfaces and let it set overnight. The next morning, wipe off soda mixture and grime, rinsing surfaces well.

- **Cutting boards** Sanitize these surfaces by spraying them with vinegar and then with 3 percent hydrogen peroxide. Keep the liquids in separate spray bottles and use them one after the other—though it doesn't matter which you use first.

Detox Tips

GreenerChoices.org, a web-based initiative dedicated to informing consumers about environmentally friendly products and practices, launched by Consumers Union, the nonprofit publisher of *Consumer Reports*, recommends avoiding cleaning products containing these substances:

- **Nonylphenol ethoxylates (NPEs)** When they're released into the environment, these chemicals can break down into toxic substances that can act as hormone disrupters, potentially threatening the reproductive capacity of fish, birds and mammals.

- **Antibacterials** Some of these may cause skin and eye irritation, and certain types, such as triclosan, may cause environmental harm by contributing to the emergence of antibiotic-resistant bacteria. Experts note that it's not the type of cleaner that matters in combating germs, but the frequency and thoroughness of cleaning—and plain soap and hot water are usually sufficient.

- **Ammonia** It is poisonous when swallowed, extremely irritating to respiratory passages when inhaled, and can burn skin on contact.

- **Butyl cellosolve** (also known as butyl glycol, ethylene glycol, monobutyl) It is poisonous when swallowed and is a lung tissue irritant.

- **Chlorine bleach (sodium hypochlorite)** It is highly irritating to the lungs and eyes.

- **D-limonene** It can irritate the skin.

- **Diethanolamine (DEA) and triethanolamine (TEA)** These chemicals can produce carcinogenic compounds, which can penetrate the skin when combined with nitrosomes, an often-undisclosed preservative or contaminant.

- **Hydrochloric acid** It can severely burn skin, and irritate the eyes and respiratory tract.

- **Naptha** This substance can cause headaches, nausea and central-nervous-system symptoms with overexposure.

- **Sodium hydroxide (lye)** It is corrosive and extremely irritating to eyes, nose and throat, and can burn those tissues on contact.

- **Sulfuric acid** It can severely damage eyes, lungs and skin.

Left: The juice of fresh lemons can be used to cut grease and remove tarnish on common metals in the kitchen, including brass, copper and aluminum.

BATHROOM

- **Tub and tile cleaner** Mix 1²/₃ cup baking soda, ½ cup liquid soap, and ½ cup water. Then add 2 tablespoons vinegar (don't add the vinegar too early or it will react with the baking soda). Immediately apply, wipe and scrub.

- **Toilet cleaner** Pour 1 cup borax into the toilet bowl before going to bed. In the morning, scrub and flush. For an extra strength cleaner, add ¼ cup vinegar to the borax.

- **Drain cleaner** First prevent clogged drains by using hair traps. To degrease and sweeten sink and tub drains, pour ½ cup of baking soda down drain, followed by 1 cup of vinegar. Let bubble for 15 minutes; rinse with hot water. You might have to repeat the procedure more than once or leave the baking soda and vinegar to "cook" overnight.

Above left: A solid-surface tub surround minimizes stains and mildew and mold growth in grout. Above right: Regularly sealing the grout between complex tile patterns helps keep it stain- and mildew-free. Right: Design Ideas' EcoGen bath accessories are biodegradable.

Resources for Cleaning Product Information

- healthyhouseinstitute.com For general information on green cleaning and other household products.
- cleaning101.com For information from the Soap and Detergent Association.
- epa.gov/iaq/molds/moldguide.html and cdc.gov/mold/strats_fungal_growth.htm For information from the U.S. Environmental Protection Agency and Centers for Disease Control and Prevention on mold prevention and remediation.
- osha.gov/SLTC/hazardcommunications/index.html For information on the Material Safety Data Sheet (MSDS), a document required by the U.S. Occupational Safety and Health Administration, which contains Lethal Dose (LD) and other toxicity data.
- leapingbunny.org For information on whether a cleaning product was tested on animals.
- greenerchoices.org For general environmental information on various cleaning products. Look at its eco-labels section to compare green claims of various household cleaners.
- panna.org For advice on nontoxic pest control solutions.
- greenseal.org For a list of cleaning products certified as environmentally friendly by Green Seal, an independent standards-making and testing body.
- watoxics.org For the Safer Cleaning Products Fact Sheet from the Washington Toxics Coalition.
- thegreenguide.com For recommendations and products reports from the Green Guide.
- householdproducts.nlm.nih.gov For safety information on brand-specific products and their ingredients listed on the National Library of Medicine's household products database.
- checnet.org/healthehouse For more safe cleaning recipes from the Children's Health Environmental Coalition.

Above: The best way to ventilate a room is to open the windows and let the fresh air flow through.

Opposite: Adding clippings from a freshly mown lawn to your compost pile will help nourish your landscape.

RECYCLING AND COMPOSTING

Every day, we all accumulate something—an empty bottle, a broken printer, yesterday's newspaper or the remains of this morning's breakfast—to toss into the garbage. But, surprisingly, about 80 percent of what Americans throw away is actually recyclable. Sadly, our recycling rate is only about 28 percent. To live as green a life as possible, before you throw anything out, whether it's an old piece of furniture, a spent lightbulb, a plastic container, an old computer or a bowlful of potato peels—try to repurpose, recycle or compost it instead. Doing so won't just make you feel better. It can actually help protect your health and the environment, too.

Recycling Household Products Containing Hazardous Substances

- **Electronic Equipment** Electronic equipment, in particular, poses an environmental hazard when disposed of in landfills, where the toxins it contains can leach into the soil and groundwater and significantly pollute the environment. Computer and CRT television monitors, for example, contain 4 to 8 lbs. of lead, which can damage a person's nervous and immune systems and kidneys. In fact, the EPA

cites electronic products as the largest single source of lead in municipal solid waste. Cell phone batteries, on the other hand, may contain cadmium, which is considered to be a carcinogen.

Thankfully, most electronic components can now be reused or recycled and kept out of the waste stream. If you have electronic equipment you no longer need, donate or recycle it through an environmentally friendly source. There are now numerous responsible recycling options for old computers, rechargeable batteries and printer cartridges. To be sure your equipment will be recycled properly, choose a recycler that has signed what is known

Recycling Resources

- **greenerchoices.org** For more information on how to safely recycle electronics and fluorescent lamps and protect your identity before recycling a computer.

- **800-424-LEAD (5323)** For more information from The National Lead Information Center on how to reduce lead hazards in your home.

- **epa.gov/epawaste/conserve/materials/ecycling/index. htm** For information from the EPA on e-waste legislation and an e-cycling map in your area. For more information about the EPA's ozone protection program, responsible appliance disposal, or to report violations, call the EPA's Stratospheric Ozone Protection Hotline toll-free at 800-296-1996.

- **epa.gov/bulbrecycling** To find a household-hazardous-waste facility near you to dispose of CFLs and other lightbulbs containing hazardous material.

- **eiae.org** For a map of e-cycling centers by state on the Electronic Industry Alliance website.

- **www.computertakeback.com** For information from the Electronics TakeBack Coalition, a national coalition of nonprofit organizations promoting responsible recycling and green design in the electronics industry.

- **ban.org** For information from the Basel Action Network on responsible recyclers.

- **rbrc.org** For information from the industry-funded Rechargeable Battery Recycling Corporation, which has more than 30,000 locations where you can drop off batteries for recycling, including many major retailers such as Best Buy, The Home Depot, Staples and Target.

as the Electronics Recycler's Pledge of True Stewardship, a voluntary commitment developed by the Basel Action Network (BAN), an environmental advocacy group focused on toxic wastes, products and technologies. These recyclers agree not to export hazardous electronic components to developing countries or dispose of equipment in municipal landfills or incinerators that aren't equipped to handle it.

- **Appliances** In addition to electronics, many of the appliances we use every day also contain man-made chemicals that destroy the ozone layer—the earth's natural protection against the sun's harmful ultraviolet radiation. Refrigerators, air conditioners and dehumidifiers, for example, depend on refrigerants containing ozone-depleting CFCs and HCFCs. If not disposed of properly at a landfill or scrap-processing facility, these common household items can release CFC/HCFC-containing refrigerants into the atmosphere. In 1990, the U.S. Congress amended the Clean Air Act to include laws to protect the stratospheric ozone layer. Part of this new law prohibits the release of ozone-depleting refrigerants into the atmosphere during the service, maintenance or disposal of air conditioners and refrigeration equipment. Since your municipality, waste hauler, scrap metal recycle company, or landfill may not own refrigerant-recovery equipment, contact the public works department in your town or county and ask about home appliance recycling or CFC/HCFC-recovery programs before disposing of refrigerant-dependent appliances. Or ask your local home appliance retailers about their refrigerator and home appliance collection programs or about the availability of refrigerant-recovery services. And let your local hauler or service person know about the ozone problem and the law—violators can be fined as much as $25,000 a day for letting refrigerant escape into the atmosphere.

- **Lightbulbs** While CFLs and other fluorescent sources are environmentally friendly for their energy efficiency and long life, they also contain small amounts of mercury, a neurotoxin, and should be recycled to prevent its release into the environment. Contact your sanitation department to see if recycling is an option in your area. Or contact the manufacturer to see if it will accept spent bulbs, as Sylvania has recently started to do (though you need to ship the bulbs to the company at your own expense). Another

possible drop-off point for lifeless lightbulbs is IKEA, the Swedish furniture retailer, whose stores now accept old bulbs. In San Francisco, the city has set up a partnership with local hardware stores to take the bulbs.

Composting

Just as you can recycle your electronics and appliances, you can also recycle your kitchen waste simply by designating separate storage containers for recyclable packaging materials, such as paper, metal, plastic and glass. The eco-friendliest approach to dealing with food scraps is to convert them into nutrient-rich compost, which can be used to nourish gardens or crops. Find out if your town has a green waste program, like San Francisco does. If so, you'll be supplied with a special bin for food and yard waste that will be taken away by your local garbage company to a municipal composting facility. If it doesn't, you can purchase a composting bin and start a composting area in your own backyard. To make an effective compost pile, you'll need to combine your kitchen fruit and vegetable scraps, coffee grounds and egg shells—known as green materials—with brown materials such as twigs, leaves, weeds and grass clippings, in the correct proportions. Ideally, this mix should include 25 percent green materials and 75 percent brown materials. Never include meat, fish or dairy products in your compost pile.

Right top and bottom: A Biostack Composter from Smith & Hawken (top) lets you turn food scraps, twigs and grass clippings into compost in your own backyard, while NatureMill's colorful under-counter composters (bottom), with built-in carbon filters, allow you to compost kitchen waste and paper in your kitchen odor-free.

VENTILATING AND CLEANING INDOOR AIR

Your home may be made of healthy materials and filled with eco-friendly furnishings and fabrics. And you may vacuum regularly and clean it with the least-toxic cleaners. But you may still feel the need for additional air filtration and cleaning to reduce the impact of airborne and biological pollutants, such as tobacco smoke, animal dander, pollen and dust, particularly if you or a family member is allergy-prone or has chemical sensitivities.

To keep indoor air fresh, the first step is to keep it properly ventilated. Because residential structures were fairly loosely built until about 50 years ago, air in houses was naturally ventilated not just through windows but through leaks in their structures, which allowed sufficient outside air to permeate inside and keep the interior air fresh, accounting for up to 3 to 4 air exchanges per hour. Unfortunately, the loose construction also kept these older homes from being energy-efficient. The residential standard set by the American Society of Heating, Refrigerating and Air-Conditioning Engineers is .35 air exchanges per hour. To achieve that standard now that homes are constructed more tightly, alternative strategies to both ventilate and filter or clean the air are needed.

Your first step should be to allow plenty of fresh air from the outside into the home. However, outdoor air can often contain allergens and other pollutants that can adversely affect many people. The EPA roughly divides pollutants in indoor air into three groups: particles, gaseous pollutants, and radon and its progeny. The EPA also recommends three strategies to reduce these indoor-air pollutants: source control, ventilation and air cleaning. You can control gaseous and radon-related pollutants when constructing or upgrading your home, or installing or upgrading your heating and cooling systems or stove and its exhaust system, and you can prevent mold and mildew with exhaust fans in bathrooms or laundry rooms. Aside from ventilating your home naturally through windows, you may also introduce fresh air through supply fans, a mechanical ventilation system, an air-to-air heat recovery or energy recovery ventilator, or a fresh-air intake system built into your forced-air system.

Once you've done what you can to control pollutants at their source and ventilate, your main concern may be introducing additional air filtration or air-cleaning devices to minimize inevitable indoor pollutants. While air cleaning may reduce the levels of certain pollutants, the EPA cautions that no air-cleaning product currently available will adequately remove all of the pollutants present in the typical indoor air environment.

There are three general types of air cleaners, which are typically classified by the method they use for removing particles of various sizes from the air: mechanical filters, electronic air cleaners, and ion generators. Hybrid units, using two or more of these removal methods, are also available. There are many types and sizes of air cleaners on the market, ranging from relatively inexpensive tabletop models to sophisticated and expensive whole-house systems, which are installed in the central heating and/or air-conditioning system. In addition, many existing home ventilation systems can be quite easily adapted to filter large particle pollutants, such as mold spores or pollen. The Filtrete Ultra Allergen Reduction Filter #1250 manufactured by 3M, for example, is commonly available at The Home Depot or Lowe's and will fit into a standard 1-inch-deep furnace filter slot. Some air cleaners are highly effective at particle removal, but others, particularly most tabletop models, are much less so. Also, air cleaners generally do not remove gaseous pollutants. Furthermore, the EPA currently does not recommend using air cleaners to reduce radon and its decay products, since the effectiveness of these devices is uncertain.

There is no universally accepted method for comparing air-cleaning devices, and, with the exception of one military standard used only to rate particle reduction by high-efficiency filters, the federal government has not published any guidelines or standards for use in determining how well

an air cleaner works in removing pollutants from indoor air. But several interested evaluators of portable air cleaning units have expressed their results as a clean air delivery rate (CADR), which can be used to compare pollutant removal rates between different devices. Filter manufacturers have also developed efficiency ratings systems, such as dust spot or arrestance systems, to measure a filter's ability to remove large particles from the air. To evaluate a filter's ability to remove small particles, the American Society of Heating, Refrigerating

A mechanical ventilation system and plenty of windows enable the tight envelope of this energy efficient home to be effectively ventilated year round.

Natural Air Freshener Recipe
Mix 1 teaspoon baking soda, 1 teaspoon vinegar (or lemon juice), and 2 cups hot water in a spray bottle, and spray in the air to remove odors.

- The Air-Conditioning, Heating, and Refrigeration Institute (AHRI) For further information on standards for induct air cleaners, contact a local heating/air-conditioning company, call AHRI at 703-524-8800 or visit *ari.org*.
- The Association of Home Appliance Manufacturers (AHAM) For information on its standard for portable air cleaners and a complete listing of all current AHAM-certified room air cleaners and their CADRs visit *cadr.org*. Or contact the AHAM by calling (800) 621-0298 or visit *aham.org*.
- *epa.gov/iaq/pubs/residair.html* For the EPA's booklet "Residential Air Cleaning Devices," which provides further information on air-cleaning devices to reduce indoor air pollutants. Also look for the EPA's "Reference Guide to Major Indoor Air Pollutants in the Home," which covers contaminants such as carbon monoxide, asbestos, biological chemicals, pesticides and other pollutants, and how to reduce exposure to them. Another worthwhile page on the EPA's site is *epa.gov/iaq/pubs/ozonegen.html*, where you'll find information on ozone generators that are sold as air cleaners, along with an assessment of their effectiveness and health consequences.
- The National Pesticide Information Center Sponsored by the EPA. To get answers about pesticides or to get selected EPA publications on pesticides, visit *npic.orst.edu* or call (800) 858-PEST (7378).
- *lungusa.org* For the American Lung Association's Air Cleaning Device fact sheet.
- Greenguard Environmental Institute (GEI), an organization dedicated to improving public health and quality of life through programs that improve indoor air, has three third-party certification programs that verify the green claims of various household products that affect indoor air quality. For a list of its approved indoor air filters, visit *greenguard.org*.

and Air-Conditioning Engineers has developed a system called the Minimum Efficiency Reporting Value (MERV), which rates filters on a scale of 1 to 16, with higher number ratings representing the more effective filters. HEPA filter systems, for example, are currently not rated, but are estimated to receive a rating of 17.

However, standards for rating particle removal by induct or portable air cleaners have been published by two private standard-setting trade organizations, the Air-Conditioning, Heating, and Refrigeration Institute (AHRI) and the Association of Home Appliance Manufacturers (AHAM). These estimate the efficiency or effectiveness of an air-cleaning device in removing particles from indoor air, and can be used for comparisons among different devices.

In addition to air-cleaning devices, other devices such as smoke alarms and carbon monoxide and radon detectors should be installed to prevent harmful gaseous pollutants from contaminating indoor air.

Above: French doors, flung wide open, allows cool, fresh air to flow freely through an upper-story bedroom, naturally ventilating the space.

Opposite: An old-fashioned ceiling fan and operable windows enable plenty of fresh air to circulate through this room during the warmer months.

ARCHITECTS AND DESIGNERS
Blueplum Design: blueplumdesign.com
Breakfast Room, The: 516-365-8500
Brian Patrick Flynn, Inc.: brianpatrickflynn.com
Eisner Design LLC: eisnerdesign.com
Elaine Griffin Interior Design: elainegriffin.com
J. Hirsch Interior Design: jhirschinteriors.com
Jessica Helgerson Interior Design: jhinteriordesign.com
Michelle Kaufmann Designs: mkd-arc.com
Otto Baat Group, LLC: ottobaat.com
Plumbob: onionflats.com
Richard Renner Architects: www.rrennerarchitects.com
WESKetch Architecture: wesketch.com
Yianni Doulis Architecture Studio, LLC: ydarchitecture.com

BOOKS AND MEDIA
Choosing Green: The Home Buyer's Guide to Good Green Homes,
    Jerry Yudelson (New Society Publishers, 2008); newsociety.com
*Home Enlightenment: Practical, Earth-Friendly Advice for Creating
    a Nurturing, Healthy, and Toxin-Free Home,* Annie B. Bond
    (Rodale, 2005); rodalestore.com
The Lazy Environmentalist, Josh Dorfman
    (Stewart, Tabori & Chang, 2007); stcbooks.com
Point Click Home: pointclickhome.com
*Prescriptions for a Healthy House: A Practical Guide for Architects, Builders
    & Homeowners* (Third Revised Edition), Paul Baker-Laporte,
    Erica Elliott and John Banta (New Society Publishers, 2008);
    newsociety.com
TreeHugger: treehugger.com
Water—Use It Wisely: wateruseitwisely.com
Your Eco-Friendly Home: Buying, Building, or Remodeling Green,
    Sid Davis (Amacom, 2008); amanet.org

BUILDERS, CONTRACTORS, DEVELOPERS
Environments For Living: environmentsforliving.com
McDonald Construction & Development Inc.: m-c-d.net

BUILDING PRODUCTS
3M: 3m.com
Aercon: aerconaac.com
AFM: afmsafecoat.com
Agristain: agristain.com
American Pride: americanpridepaint.com
American Standard: americanstandard-us.com
Andersen: andersenwindows.com
Avonite: avonitesurfaces.com
Bark House: barkhouse.com
BioShield : bioshieldpaint.com
CaesarStone: caesarstoneus.com
Cambria Quartz: cambriausa.com
Cargill BiOH polyols: bioh.com

Caroma: caromausa.com
CertainTeed: certainteed.com
Christiana Cabinetry: christianacabinetry.com
Cob Cottage Company: cobcottage.com
Contec: contecinc.com
Corian: dupont.com
DuPont: dupont.com
Durisol: durisolbuild.com
Eagle Roofing Products: eagleroofing.com
EcoSmart Fire: ecosmartfire.com
Elmer's Carpenter Glue: elmers.com
EnviroGLAS: enviroglasproducts.com
Faswall: faswall.com
Formica: formica.com
Humabuilt HumaBlock: humabuilt.com
IceStone: icestone.biz
Jeld-Wen: jeld-wen.com
Knauf Insulation: knaufusa.com
Marvin: marvin.com
Moen: moen.com
Nevamar: nevamar.com
PaperStone: paperstoneproducts.com
Pittsburgh Paints: pittsburghpaints.com
Richlite: richlite.com
Sherwin-Williams: sherwin-williams.com
Silestone: silestoneusa.com
Squak Mountain Stone: squakmountainstone.com
Swanstone: swanstoneproducts.com
Trespa: trespa.com
TruStone: tru-stone.com
Tyvek: dupont.com
Vetrazzo: vetrazzo.com
Weather-Bos: weatherbos.com
Wilsonart: wilsonart.com
Zodiaq: dupont.com

CLEANING, COMPOSTING AND PEST CONTROL
Biokleen: biokleenhome.com
Bora-Care: nisuscorp.com
EcoGen: ecogenlife.com
Maison Belle: isabellasmith.co.uk
NatureMill: naturemill.com

FURNITURE, SOFT GOODS AND ACCENTS MANUFACTURERS
American Drew: americandrew.com
American Home Furnishings: americanhome.com
Benjamin Moore: benjaminmoore.com
Bernhardt: bernhardt.com
Caperton: capertonfurnitureworks.com
Cisco Brothers: ciscobrothers.com

C.R. Laine Furniture: crlaine.com
Gat Creek: gatcreek.com
Hickory Chair: hickorychair.com
Ikea: ikea.com
Kincaid: kincaidfurniture.com
La-Z-Boy: la-z-boy.com
Lee Furniture: leeindustries.com
Lulan Artisans: lulan.com
Old Wood Co., The: theoldwoodco.com
Pure Furniture Design: purebyamimckay.com
Ralph Lauren Home: ralphlaurenhome.com
Rowe Furniture: rowefurniture.com
Sauder: sauder.com
Selamat: selamatdesigns.com
Stanley: stanleyfurniture.com
Valley Forge Fabrics: valleyforge.com
Vaughan: vaughandesigns.com; vaughanfurniture.com
Vaughan-Bassett: vaughan-bassett.com

GOVERNMENT AGENCIES, DATABASES AND PROGRAMS

Energy Star program: energystar.gov
Federal Trade Commission (FTC): ftc.gov
Federal Trade Commission's Energy Guide: ftc.gov/bcp/conline/edcams/eande/index.html
Household Products Database: householdproducts.nlm.nih.gov
National Lead Information Center: epa.gov/lead/pubs/nlic.htm
United States Department of Agriculture: usda.gov
U.S. Department of Energy: doe.gov
U.S. Department of Energy's Energy Efficiency and Renewable Energy: eere.energy.gov/consumer
U.S. Environmental Protection Agency: epa.gov
U.S. EPA's eCycling: epa.gov/epawaste/conserve/materials/ecycling/index.htm
U.S. EPA's Water Sense program: epa.gov/watersense
U.S. Green Building Council: usgbc.org
U.S. National Library of Medicine: nlm.nih.gov
U.S. Occupational Safety and Health Administration: osha.gov
Washington Toxics Coalition: watoxics.org

INSTRUMENTS

BioElectric Shield: bioelectricshield.com
Davis Instruments: davisnet.com
Weather Trak: weathertrak.com

ONLINE RETAILERS

EcoNest Building Company: econest.com
EcoSource Home & Garden: ecosourceonline.com
Green Building: greenbuilding.com
Green Building Resource Guide: greenguide.com
Green Depot: greendepot.com

GreenHomeGuide: greenhomeguide.com
Habitat ReStore: habitat.org/env/restore.aspx
Healthy Buildings Made Easy: healthybuildingsmadeeasy.com
Home Depot, The: homedepot.com
iGreenBuild: igreenbuild.com
Low Impact Living: lowimpactliving.com
NaturalHandyman: naturalhandyman.com
NatureWood: westernwoodpreserving.com
Organic Bouquet: organicbouquet.com
Smith & Hawken: smithandhawken.com
VeriFlora: veriflora.com
Whole Foods: wholefoodsmarket.com

PROFESSIONAL ASSOCIATIONS AND NONPROFIT ORGANIZATIONS

Air-Conditioning, Heating & Refrigeration Institute: ari.org
Alliance for Climate Protection: wecansolveit.org
Alliance to Save Energy: ase.org
American Home Furnishings Alliance: ahfa.us
American Home Furnishings Alliance's Enhancing Furniture's Environmental Culture program: ahfa.us/resources/efec/index.htm
American Home Furnishings Alliance's Sustainable by Design program: sustainablebydesign.us
American Institute of Architects: aia.org
American Lung Association: lungusa.org; healthhouse.org
American Society of Dowsers: dowsers.org
American Society of Interior Designers: asid.org
American Solar Energy Society: ases.org
American Tree Farm System: treefarmsystem.org
American Wind Energy Association: awea.org
Association of Home Appliance Manufacturers: aham.org
Asthma and Allergy Foundation of America: aafa.org
Basel Action Network: ban.org
BuildingGreen: buildinggreen.com
Build It Green: builditgreen.org
California Air Resources Board (CARB): arb.ca.gov
Carpet and Rug Institute: carpet-rug.org
Children's Health Environmental Coalition: checnet.org
Coalition for Consumer Information on Cosmetics: leapingbunny.org
Consumer Report's Greener Choices: greenerchoices.org
Database of State Incentives for Renewables & Efficiency: dsireusa.org
Earth Advantage: earthadvantage.com
EarthCraft House: earthcrafthouse.com
E-Cycling Central: eiae.org
EfficientProducts: efficientproducts.org
Electronic Industries Alliance: eia.org
Electronics TakeBack Coalition: www.computertakeback.com
Energy & Environmental Building Association: eeba.org
Environmental Working Group: ewg.org
Forest Stewardship Council: fscus.org; fsc.org

Get Energy Active: getenergyactive.org
Green-e: green-e.org
Greenguard Environmental Institute (GEI): greenguard.org
Green Media Toolshed: scorecard.org
Green Seal: greenseal.org
Healthy Building Network: healthybuilding.net
Healthy House Institute: healthyhouseinstitute.com
Institute of Marketecology (IMO): imo.ch
International Institute for Bau-Biologie & Ecology: bau-biologieusa.com
Kitchen Cabinet Manufacturers Association: kcma.org;
    greencabinetsource.org
Malaysian Timber Certification Council: mtcc.com.my
National Association of Home Builders: nahb.org
National Association of the Remodeling Industry: nari.org
National Fenestration Rating Council: nfrc.org
Metafore: metafore.org
Metal Initiative: themetalinitiative.com
Metal Roofing Alliance: metalroofing.com
National Pesticide Information Center: npic.orst.edu
National Sanitation Foundation: nsf.org
National Wildlife Federation: nwf.org
Natural Resources Defense Council: nrdc.org
North American Insulation Manufacturers Association: naima.org;
    simplyinsulate.com
Pan North America: panna.org
Partnership for Advancing Technology in Housing: pathnet.org
Rechargeable Battery Recycling Corporation: rbrc.org
Resilient Floor Covering Institute: rfci.com
Rohm and Haas Paint Quality Institute: paintquality.com
Scientific Certification Systems: scscertified.com
Soap and Detergent Association: cleaning101.com
Sustainable by Design: susdesign.com
Sustainable Forestry Initiative, Inc.: sfiprogram.org
Sustainable Furnishings Council: sustainablefurniturecouncil.org
Swiss Accreditation Service (SAS): www.seco.admin.ch/sas/
    index.html?lang=en
ToolBase Services: toolbase.org
Vinyl Institute: vinylinfo.org
Western Red Cedar: wrcla.org
World Floor Covering Association: wfca.org

ACKNOWLEDGMENTS

The talent and aid of several people went into the development of this book and all deserve our acknowledgment and gratitude.

Several architects and designers shared their insight as well as photographs of their work and without their support this book would not have been possible. Chief among them are Eve Blossom, Yianni Doulis, Joseph Eisner, Brian Flynn, Anastasia Harrison, Jessica Helgerson, Pamela Hill, Janie Hirsch, Michelle Kaufmann, Scott Lois Mackenzie, Martin, Michael and Timothy McDonald, Rick Renner and Vasi Ypsilantis.
We would also like to thank the many photographers who contributed to the creation of this book, including Lincoln Barbour, Sarah Dorio, Casey Dunn, John Gruen, David Groul, Ken Gutmaker, Rob Kern, Chris Little, Mariko Reed, Jamie Solomon, David Duncan Livingston, Steven Mays, Keith Scott Morton, Michael Partenio, Marisa Pellegrini, Jay Rosenblatt, Susan Sully, John Swain and Paul Warchol.
Our very special thanks go to Kathy Ritchie for her product photo research, as well as to Matthew Levinson, Christine Cameron and Ayn-Monique Tetreault-Rooney for their production assistance. Much of the research for this book was drawn from numerous books, professional, nonprofit, and government sources and websites, which are listed in the resource guide or bibliography at the end of this book.
Finally, we would like to express our gratitude to Dorothée Walliser for her support of our vision for this book as well as her gracious and talented efforts in seeing it through to publication.

Websites, prices and contact information listed in this book are accurate at the time of publication, but they are subject to frequent change.